Who Should Read This Book?

We've all heard the scenario: the family on vacation stops at a road-side "dig your own" gem mine. Junior finds a sapphire the size of a peach and ends up on national television telling the world how he will spend his fortune.

↑ This book is for those who have read these stories and want their chance to find their own fortune. It is also a book for those who would enjoy the adventure of finding a few gems, getting them cut or polished, and making their own jewelry. It is a book for those people who want to plan a gem hunting vacation with their family. It is a book for those who study the metaphysical properties of gems and minerals and would like to add to their personal collections.

↑ This book is for those who would like to keep the art of rock-hounding alive and pass it on to their children. It is a book on where to find your own gems and minerals and on how to begin what for many is a lifelong hobby.

↑ This is a book for those who aren't interested in the "hidden treasure map through mosquito-infested no-man's-land" approach to treasure hunting but do want to find gems and minerals. It is for those who want to get out the pick and shovel and get a little dirty. (Although at some mines they bring the buckets of pre-dug dirt to you at an environmentally temper-ature controlled sluicing area.)

Many an unsuspecting tourist has stopped at a mine to try his or her luck and become a rockhound for life. Watch out! Your collection may end up taking the place of your car in your garage.

Good hunting!

This volume is one in a four-volume series.

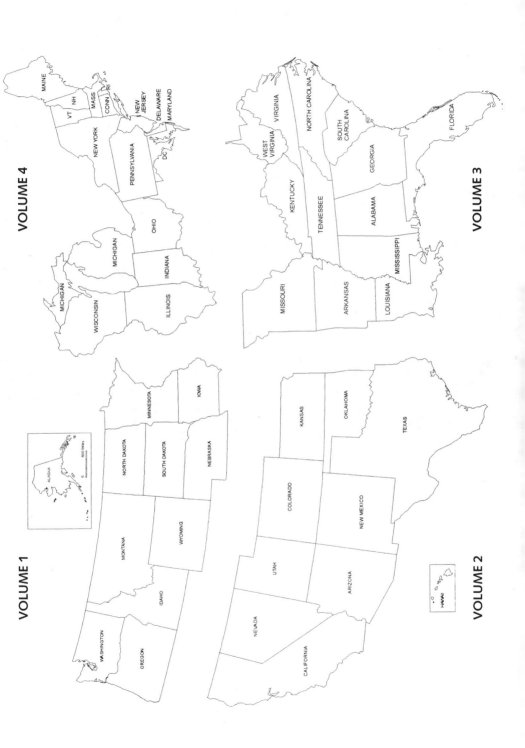

VOLUME 4

VOLUME 1

VOLUME 3

VOLUME 2

The Treasure Hunter's

GEM & MINERAL GUIDES TO THE U.S.A.

Where & How to Dig, Pan, and Mine Your Own Gems & Minerals

VOLUME 3: SOUTHEAST STATES

by KATHY J. RYGLE AND STEPHEN F. PEDERSEN
Preface by Antoinette L. Matlins, P.G.,
author of *Gem Identification Made Easy*

GemStone Press • Woodstock, Vermont

The Treasure Hunter's Gem & Mineral Guides to the U.S.A.: Where & How to Dig,
Pan, and Mine Your Own Gems & Minerals
Volume 3: Southeast States

Copyright © 1999 by Kathy J. Rygle and Stephen F. Pedersen
Preface © Antoinette L. Matlins

Library of Congress Cataloging-in-Publication Data
Rygle, Kathy J., 1955–
 Treasure hunter's gem & mineral guides to the U.S.A. : where & how to dig, pan,
 and mine your own gems & minerals / Kathy J. Rygle and Stephen F. Pedersen.
  p. cm.
 Includes index.
 Contents: [1] Northwest region — [2] Southwest region — [3] Northeast
 region — [4] Southeast region.
  ISBN 0-943763-24-X (pbk. : NW). — ISBN 0-943763-25-8 (pbk. : SW). —
 ISBN 0-943763-27-4 (pbk. : NE). — ISBN 0-943763-26-6 (pbk. : SE)
  1. Minerals—United States—Collection and preservation Guidebooks.
 2. Precious stones—United States—Collection and preservation Guidebooks.
 3. United States Guidebooks.
  I. Pedersen, Stephen F., 1948– . II. Title. III. Title: Treasure hunter's gem
 and mineral guides to the U.S.A.
 QE375.R94 1999
 549.973—dc21   99-39215
                                               CIP

Cover design by Bronwen Battaglia
Text design by Chelsea Dippel

10 9 8 7 6 5 4 3 2 1

Published by GemStone Press
A Division of LongHill Partners, Inc.
Sunset Farm Offices, Route 4
P.O. Box 237
Woodstock, VT 05091
Tel: (802) 457-4000   Fax: (802) 457-4004
www.gemstonepress.com

Dedications, with love, to our parents and children:

To my parents, Joe and Helen Rygle, who taught me the love of nature; my earliest remembrances of "rockhounding" are hikes with my dad in the fields, forests, and streams near our home. I also remember weekend trips with my mother to a shop that sold specimens of minerals from around the world. To my daughter, Annie Rygle, who shares with me and continues to show me the wonders of nature.   —K.J.R.

To my parents, Cliff and Leone Pedersen, who taught me to value nature and to not quit. To my daughters Kristi and Debbie, who challenge me to keep growing.   —S.F.P.

To our combined families, including Georgia Pedersen, and to family no longer with us.

With special thanks:

To all the owners of fee dig mines and guide services, curators and staff of public and private museums, mine owners, and miners. Our thanks to all those individuals both past and present who share the wonders of the earth with us.

To our agent, Barb Doyen, and her childhood rock collection.

To our publisher, Stuart Matlins, editor Sandra Korinchak, and all the staff at GemStone Press for their guidance, assistance, and patience.

To Mrs. Betty Jackson for, in her own way, telling Kathy to write the book.

To God and the wonders He has given us.

And finally, to each other, with love and the perseverance to keep on trying.

Volume 3—Southeast States

CONTENTS

PREFACE

All-American Gems

by Antoinette L. Matlins, P.G.

When Americans think of costly and fabled gems, they associate them with exotic origins—Asia, South Africa or Brazil. They envision violent jungle quests or secret cellars of a sultanate, perhaps scenes from a Jorge Amado novel or from *A Thousand and One Nights,* a voluptuous Indian princess whose sari is adorned with the plentiful rubies and sapphires of her land, or a Chinese emperor sitting atop a throne flanked by dragons carved from exquisitely polished jade.

Asked what gems are mined in the United States, most Americans would probably draw a blank. We know our country is paved with one of the finest highway systems in the world, but we don't know that just below the surface, and sometimes on top of it, is a glittering pavement of gemstones that would color Old Glory. The red rubies of North Carolina, the white diamonds of Arkansas, the blue sapphires of Montana—America teems with treasures that its citizens imagine come from foreign lands. These include turquoise, tourmaline, amethyst, pearls, opals, jade, sapphires, emeralds, rubies, and even gem-quality diamonds.

Not only does America have quantity, it has quality. American gems compare very favorably with gems from other countries. In fact, fine gemstones found in the U.S. can rival specimens from anywhere else in the world. Some gems, like the luxurious emerald-green hiddenite and steely blue benitoite, are found only in America. Others, like the tourmalines of Maine and California, rival specimens found in better-known locations such as Brazil and Zambia.

The discovery of gemstones in U.S. terrain has been called a lost chapter in American history. It continues to be a saga of fashion and fable that, like the stones themselves, are a deep part of our national heritage. Appreciation of our land's generous yield of sparkling colored stones reached a zenith at the end of the nineteenth century with the art nouveau movement and its utilization of them. When the Boer Wars ended, South Africa's diamonds and platinum eclipsed many of our own then so-called semiprecious stones. Not until the 1930s and again starting with the 1960s, did economics and the yen for color make gems more desirable again.

In the late 1800s, the nation sought out and cherished anything that was unique to the land. The search for gemstones in America coincided with the exploration of the West, and nineteenth-century mineralogists, some bonafide and others self-proclaimed, fulfilled that first call for "Made in America." Their discoveries created sensations not only throughout America but in the capitals of Europe and as far away as China. The Europeans, in fact, caught on before the Americans, exhibiting some of America's finest specimens in many of Europe's great halls.

But the search for gemstones in this country goes back even further than the nineteenth century. In 1541, the Spanish explorer Francisco Coronado trekked north from Mexico in the footsteps of Cortés and Pizarro, searching not only for gold but also for turquoise, amethyst and emeralds. In the early 1600s, when English settlers reached Virginia, they had been instructed "to searche for gold and such jeweles as ye may find."

But what eluded the Spanish explorers and early settlers was unearthed by their descendants. Benitoite, which may be our nation's most uniquely attractive gem, was discovered in 1907 in California's San Benito River headwaters. A beautiful, rare gem with the color of fine sapphire and the fire of a diamond, benitoite is currently found in gem quality only in San Benito, California.

Like many of America's finest stones discovered during the "Gem Rush" of the nineteenth century, benitoite was held in higher regard throughout the rest of the world than it was on its native U.S. soil.

The gem occurs most commonly in various shades of blue. A fine-quality blue benitoite can resemble fine blue sapphire, but it is even more brilliant. It has one weakness, however: in comparison to sapphire, it is relatively soft. It is therefore best used in pendants, brooches and earrings, or in rings with a protective setting.

While benitoite is among the rarest of our gems, our riches hardly stop there. America is the source of other unusual gems, including three even more uniquely American stones, each named after an American: kunzite, hiddenite and morganite.

The story of all-American kunzite is inseparable from the achievements of two men: Charles Lewis Tiffany, founder of Tiffany & Co., and Dr. George Frederick Kunz, world-renowned gemologist. By seeking, collecting and promoting gems found in America, these two did more for the development of native stones than anyone else during, or since, their time.

While working for Tiffany in the late 1800s, Dr. Kunz received a package in the mail containing a stone that the sender believed to be an unusual tourmaline. The stone came from an abandoned mine at Pala Mountain, California, where collectors had found traces of spodumene—a gemstone prized by the ancients but which no one had been able to find for many years. Dr. Kunz was ecstatic to find before him a specimen of "extinct spodumene of a gloriously lilac color." A fellow gemologist, Dr. Charles Baskerville, named the find "kunzite" in his honor.

Kunzite has become a favorite of such designers as Paloma Picasso, not only because of its distinctive shades lilac, pink, and yellow-green orchid—but because it is one of a diminishing number of gems available in very large sizes at affordable prices. It is a perfect choice for the centerpiece around which to create a very bold, dramatic piece of jewelry. Designer Picasso's creations include a magnificent necklace using a 400-carat kunzite. Although it is a moderately hard stone, kunzite is easily fractured, and care must be taken to avoid any sharp blows.

Kunzite's sister gem, hiddenite, is also a truly "all-American" stone. In 1879, William Earl Hidden, an engraver and mineralogist, was sent to North Carolina on behalf of the great American inventor and prospector Thomas Alva Edison to search for platinum. Hidden found none of the precious white metal but in his pursuit unearthed a new green gemstone, which was named "hiddenite" in his honor.

Less well known than kunzite, hiddenite is an exquisite, brilliant emerald-green variety of spodumene not found anyplace else in the world. While light green and yellow-green shades have been called hiddenite, the Gemological Institute of America—this country's leading authority on gemstones—considers only the emerald-green shade of spodumene, found exclusively in the Blue Ridge Mountains of Mitchell County, North Carolina, to be true hiddenite.

The foothills of the Blue Ridge Mountains also possess America's most significant emerald deposits. While output is minimal compared to Colombia, Zambia or Pakistan, the Rist Mine in Hiddenite, North Carolina, has produced some very fine emeralds, comparable to Colombian stones. The discovery was first made by a farmer plowing his field who found them lying loose on the soil. The country folk, not knowing what they had come across, called the stones "green bolts."

In August 1970, a 26-year-old "rock hound" named Wayne Anthony found a glowing 59-carat "green bolt" at the Rist Mine only two feet from the surface. It was cut into a 13.14-carat emerald of very fine color. Tiffany & Co. later purchased the stone and called it the Carolina Emerald. "The gem is superb," said Paul E. Desautels, then the curator of mineralogy at the Smithsonian Institution. "It can stand on its own merits as a fine and lovely gem of emerald from anywhere, including Colombia." In 1973, the emerald became the official state stone of North Carolina.

A California prize, the warm peach- or pink-shaded morganite, was named by Dr. Kunz for financier John Pierpont Morgan, who purchased the Bement gem collection for donation to the American Museum of Natural History in New York, where it can be viewed today. Morganite is a member of the beryl family, which gives us aquamarine (the clear blue variety of beryl) and emerald (the deep green variety of beryl). However, morganite is available in much larger sizes than its mineralogical cousins and is much more affordable.

Many consider the core of our national treasure chest to be gems like the tourmalines of Maine and California and the sapphires of Montana, gems that are mined in commercial quantities and have earned worldwide reputations. One day in the fall of 1820, two young boys, Ezekiel Holmes and Elijah Hamlin, were rock hunting on Mount Mica in Oxford County, Maine. On the way home, one of the boys saw a flash of green light coming from underneath an uprooted tree. The find was later identified as tourmaline, and Mount Mica became the site of the first commercial gem mine in the United States. The mine was initially worked by Elijah Hamlin and his brother Hannibal, who later became Abraham Lincoln's vice president.

The colors of the rainbow meld delicately in the tourmalines of Maine, producing some of the finest specimens in the world, rivaling in quality even those from Brazil. A 150-mile strip in central Maine provides shades of apple green, burgundy red and salmon pink, to mention just a few. Some stones are bi-colored.

Miners are kept busy in the Pala district of San Diego County, California, as well. California, in fact, is North America's largest producer of gem-quality tourmaline.

The hot-pink tourmalines, for which California is famous, began to come into greater demand in 1985, as pastel-colored stones became more and more coveted by chic women around the globe. Curiously enough, over one hundred years ago the Chinese rejoiced in the fabulous colors of this fashionable stone. The Empress Dowager of the Last Chinese Imperial Dynasty sent emissaries to California in search of pink tourmalines. She garnished her robes with carved tourmaline buttons and toggles, and started a fad which overtook China. Much of the empress's collection of fine carvings was lost or stolen when the dynasty fell around 1912, but artifacts made from California's pink tourmaline can be seen today in a Beijing museum. China's fascination with pink tourmalines lasted long after the empress. In 1985, a contingent of the Chinese Geological Survey came to California with two requests: to see Disneyland and the Himalaya Mine, original site of California pink tourmaline.

While the Chinese are mesmerized by our tourmalines, Americans have always been attracted to China's jade. But perhaps we ought to take stock of our own. Wyoming, in fact, is the most important producer of the stone in the Western Hemisphere. The state produces large quantities of good-quality green nephrite jade—the type most commonly used in jewelry and carvings. California also boasts some jade, as does Alaska. Chinese immigrants panning for gold in California in the late 1800s found large boulders of nephrite and sent them back to China, where the jade was carved and sold within China and around the world.

The U.S. is also one of the largest producers of turquoise. Americans mostly associate this stone with American Indian jewelry, but its use by mainstream designers has regularly come in and out of fashion.

Some of the most prized gems of America are the stunning sapphires from Yogo Gulch, Montana. These sapphires emit a particularly pleasing shade of pale blue, and are known for their clarity and brilliance.

The Montana mine was originally owned by a gold-mining partnership. In 1895, an entire summer's work netted a total of only $700 in gold plus a cigar box full of heavy blue stones. The stones were sent to Tiffany & Co. to be identified. Tiffany then sent back a check for $3,750 for the entire box of obviously valuable stones.

Once one can conceive of gem-quality sapphires in America, it takes only a small stretch of the mind to picture the wonderful diamonds found here. A 40.23-carat white gem found in Murfreesboro, Arkansas was cut into a 14.42-carat emerald-cut diamond named Uncle Sam. Other large diamonds include a 23.75 carat diamond found in the mid-nineteenth century in Manchester, Virginia, and a greenish 34.46-carat diamond named the Punch Jones, which was claimed to have been found in Peterstown, West Virginia.

Each year, thousands of people visit Crater of Diamonds State Park in Arkansas, where, for a fee, they can mine America's only proven location of gem-quality diamonds. Among them is a group known as "regulars" who visit the park looking for their "retirement stone."

In 1983, one of the regulars, 82-year-old Raymond Shaw, came across a 6.7-carat rough diamond. He sold it for $15,000 uncut. According to Mark Myers, assistant superintendent of the state park, the stone was cut into an exceptionally fine, 2.88 carat gem (graded E/Flawless by the Gemological Institute of America). Myers says the cut stone, later called the Shaw Diamond, was offered for sale for $58,000.

Diamonds have also been found along the shores of the Great Lakes, in many localities in California, in the Appalachian Mountains, in Illinois, Indiana, Ohio, Kentucky, New York, Idaho and Texas. Exploration for diamonds continues in Michigan, Wisconsin, Colorado and Wyoming, according to the U.S. Bureau of Mines. The discovery of gem-quality diamonds in Alaska in 1986 initiated a comprehensive search there for man's most valued gem.

Many questions concerning this country's store of gems remain unanswered. "Numerous domestic deposits of semiprecious gem stones are known and have been mined for many years," wrote the Bureau of Mines in a 1985 report. "However, no systematic evaluations of the magnitude of these deposits have been made and no positive statements can be made about them." Even as the United States continues to offer up its kaleidoscopic range of gems, our American soil may hold a still greater variety and quantity of gems yet to be unearthed.

And here, with the help of these down-to-earth (in the best possible way!)

guides, you can experience America's gem and mineral riches for yourself. In these pages rockhounds, gemologists, vacationers, and families alike will find a hands-on introduction to the fascinating world of gems and minerals . . . and a treasure map to a sparkling side of America. Happy digging!

T

Antoinette L. Matlins, P.G. is an internationally respected gem and jewelry expert, author and lecturer. Active in the gem trade and a popular media guest, she has been seen on ABC, CBS, NBC, and CNN, educating consumers about gems and jewelry and exposing fraud. Her books include *Jewelry & Gems: The Buying Guide, 4th Edition; Engagement & Wedding Rings, 2nd Edition: The Definitive Buying Guide for People in Love; The Pearl Book: The Definitive Buying Guide;* and *Gem Identification Made Easy, 2nd Edition: A Hands-On Guide to More Confident Buying & Selling* (GemStone Press).

Introduction

This is a guide to commercially operated gem and mineral mines (fee dig mines) within the United States that offer would-be treasure hunters the chance to "dig their own," from diamonds to thundereggs.

For simplicity, the term *fee dig site* is used to represent all types of fee-based mines or collection sites. However, for liability reasons, many mines no longer let collectors dig their own dirt, but rather dig it for them and provide it in buckets or bags. Some fee-based sites involve surface collection.

This book got its start when the authors, both environmental scientists, decided to make their own wedding rings. Having heard stories about digging your own gems, they decided to dig their own stones for their rings. So off to Idaho and Montana they went, taking their three children, ages 8, 13, and 15 at the time, in search of opals and garnets, their birthstones. They got a little vague information before and during the trip on where to find gem mines and in the process got lost in some of those "mosquito-infested lands." But when they did find actual "dig your own" mines (the kind outlined in this book), they found opals, garnets, and even sapphires. They have since made other trips to fee dig mines and each time have come home with treasures and some incredible memories.

The authors are also now the proud owners of a set of lapidary equipment, i.e., rock saw and rock polisher. They first used them to cut thundereggs collected from a mine in Oregon. The next project was to trim the many pounds of fossil fish rocks they acquired at a fee dig fossil site. The sequel to this guide series will cover authorized fossil collecting sites as well as museums on fossils and dinosaurs. It will include such topics as where to view and even make plaster casts of actual dinosaur tracks. There are even museums where kids of all ages can dig up a full-sized model of a dinosaur!

Types of Sites

The purpose of this book is principally to guide the reader to fee dig mine sites. These are gem or mineral mines where you hunt for the gem or mineral in ore at or from the mine. At fee dig sites where you are actually permitted to go into the field and dig for yourself, you will normally be shown what the gem or mineral you are seeking looks like in its natural state (much different from the polished or cut stone). Often someone is available to go out in the field with you and show you where to dig. At sites where you purchase gem- or mineral-bearing ore (either native or enriched) for washing in a flume, the process is the same: there will usually be examples of rough stones for comparison, and help in identifying your finds.

Also included are a few areas that are not fee dig sites but that are well-defined collecting sites, usually parks or beaches.

Guided field trips are a little different. Here the guide may or may not have examples of what you are looking for, but he or she will be with you in the field to help in identifying finds.

For the more experienced collector, there are field collecting areas where you are on your own in identifying what you have found. Several fee areas and guided field trips appropriate for the experienced collector are available. Check out the listings for Ruggles Mine (Grafton, NH); Harding Mine (Dixon, NM); Poland Mining Camps (Poland, ME); Perhams (West Paris, ME); and Gem Mountain Quarry Trips (Spruce Pine, NC).

Knowing What You're Looking For

Before you go out into the field, it is a good idea to know what you are looking for. Most of the fee dig mines listed in this guide will show you specimens before you set out to find your own. If you are using a guide service, you have the added bonus of having a knowledgeable person with you while you search to help you find the best place to look and help you identify your finds.

Included here is a listing of museums that contain rock and gem exhibits. A visit to these museums will help prepare you for your search. You may find examples of gems in the rough and examples of mineral specimens similar to the ones you will be looking for. Museums will most likely have displays of gems or minerals native to the local area. Some of the gems and minerals listed in this guide are of significant interest, and specimens of them can be found in museums around the country. Displays accompanying the exhibits might tell you how the gems and minerals were found, and their place in our nation's history. Many museum also hold collecting field trips or geology programs, or may be able to put you in touch with local rock and lapidary clubs.

For more information on learning how to identify your finds yourself—and even how to put together a basic portable "lab" to use at the sites—the book *Gem Identification Made Easy* by A.L. Matlins and A.C. Bonanno (Gem-Stone Press) is a good resource.

Rock shops are another excellent place to view gems and mineral specimens before going out to dig your own. A listing of rock shops would be too extensive to include in a book such as this. A good place to get information on rock shops in the area you plan to visit is to contact the chamber of commerce for that area. Rock shops may be able to provide information not only on rockhounding field trips but also on local rock clubs that sponsor trips.

Through mine tours you can see how minerals and gems were and are taken from the earth. On these tours, visitors learn what miners go through to remove the ores from the earth. This will give you a better appreciation for those sparkly gems you see in the showroom windows, and for many of the items we all take for granted in daily use.

You will meet other rockhounds at the mine. Attending one of the yearly events listed in the guide will also give you the chance to meet people who share your interest in gems and minerals and exchange ideas, stories, and knowledge of the hobby.

How to Use This Guide

To use this book, you can pick a state and determine what mining is available there, or pick a gem or mineral and determine where to go to "mine" it.

In this guide are indexes that will make the guide simple to use. If you are interested in finding a particular gem or mineral, go to the Index by Gem or Mineral in the back of the book. In this index, gems and minerals are listed in alphabetical order with the states and cities where fee dig sites for that gem or mineral may be found.

If you are interested in learning of sites near where you live, or in the area where you are planning a vacation, or if you simply want to know whether there are gems and minerals in a particular location, go to the Index by State, located in the back of the guide. The state index entries are broken down into three categories: Fee Dig Sites/Guide Services, Museums and Mine Tours, and Special Events and Tourist Information.

There are also several special indexes for use in finding your birthstone, anniversary stone, or zodiac stone.

Site Listings

The first section of each chapter lists fee dig sites and guide services that are available in each state. Included with the location of each site is a description of the site, directions to find it, what equipment is provided, and what you must supply. Costs are listed, along with specific policies of the site. Also included are other services available at the site and information on camping, lodging, etc. in the area of the site. Included in the section with fee dig sites are guide services for collecting gems and minerals.

In the second section of each chapter, museums of special interest to the gem/mineral collector and mine tours available to the public are listed. Besides being wonderful ways to learn about earth science, geology, and mining history (many museums and tours also offer child-friendly exhibits), museums are particularly useful for viewing gems and minerals in their rough or natural state before going out in the field to search for them.

The third section of each chapter lists special events involving gems and minerals, and resources for general tourist information.

A sample of the listings for fee dig mines and guide services (Section 1 in the guides) is on the next page.

Tips for mining:

1. Learn what gems or minerals can be found at the mine you are going to visit.
2. Know what the gem or mineral that you're hunting looks like in the rough before you begin mining.

Visiting local rock shops and museums will help in this effort.
3. When in doubt, save any stone that you are unsure about. Have an expert at the mine or at a local rock shop help you identify your find.

Sample Fee Dig Site Listing

TOWN in which the site is located / *Native or enriched[1] • Easy, moderate, difficult[2]*

Dig your own *T*

The following gems may be found:
- List of gems and minerals found at the mine

Mine name
Owner or contact (where available)
Address
Phone number
Fax
E-mail address
Website address

Open: months, hours, days
Info: Descriptive text regarding the site, including whether equipment is provided.
Admission: Fee to dig; costs for predug dirt
Other services available
Other area attractions (at times)
Information on lodging or campground facilities (where available)
Directions

Map (where available)

Notes:

1. Native or enriched. *Native* refers to gems or minerals found in the ground at the site, put there by nature. *Enriched* means that gems and minerals from an outside source have been brought in and added to the soil. Enriching is also called "salting"—it is a guaranteed return. Whatever is added in a salted mine is generally the product of some commercial mine elsewhere. Thus, it is an opportunity to "find" gemstones from around the world the easy way, instead of traveling to jungles and climbing mountains in remote areas of the globe. Salted mines are particularly nice for giving children the opportunity to find a wide variety of gems and become involved in gem identification. The authors have tried to indicate if a mine is enriched, but to be sure, ask at the mine beforehand. If the status could not be determined, this designation was left out.

2. Sites are designated as easy, moderate, or difficult. This was done to give you a feel for what a site may be like. You should contact the site and make a determination for yourself if you have any doubts.

Easy: This might be a site where the gem hunter simply purchases bags or buckets of predug dirt, washes the ore in a flume or screens the gem-bearing gravel to concentrate the gems, and flips the screen. The gems or minerals are then picked out of the material remaining in the screen. A mine which has set aside a pile of mine material for people to pick through would be another type of site designated as "Easy."

Moderate: Mining at a "Moderate" site might mean digging with a shovel, then loading the dirt into buckets, followed by sifting and sluicing. Depending on your knowledge of mineral identification, work at a "Moderate" site might include searching the surface of the ground at an unsupervised area for a gem or mineral you are not familiar with (this could also be considered difficult).

Difficult: This might be a site requiring tools such as picks and shovels, or sledge hammers and chisels. The site may be out of the way and/or difficult to get to. Mining might involve heavy digging with the pick and shovel or breaking gems or minerals out of base rock using a sledge or chisel.

Special Note:

Although most museums and many fee dig sites are handicapped accessible, please check with the listing directly.

Maps

Maps are included to help you locate the sites in the guide. At the beginning of each state, there is a state map showing the general location of towns where sites are located.

Local maps are included in a listing when the information was available. *These maps are not drawn to scale!* These maps provide information to help you get to the site but are not intended to be a substitute for a road map. Please check directly with the site you are interested in for more detailed directions.

Fees

Fees listed in these guides were obtained when the book was compiled, and may have changed. They are included to give you at least a general idea of the costs you will be dealing with. Please contact the site directly to confirm charges.

Many museums have discounts for members and for groups, as well as special programs for school groups. Please check directly with the institution for information. Many smaller and/or private institutions have no fee, but do appreciate donations to help meet the costs of staying open.

Many sites accept credit cards; some may not. Please check ahead for payment options if this is important.

Requesting Information by Mail

When requesting information by mail, it is always appreciated if you send a SASE (self-addressed stamped envelope) along with your request. Doing this will often speed up the return of information.

Equipment and Safety Precautions

Equipment

The individual sites listed in these guides often provide equipment at the mine. Please note that some fee dig sites place limitations on the equipment you can use at their site. Those limitations will be noted where the information was available. Always abide by the limitations; remember that you are a guest at the site.

On the following pages are figures showing equipment for rockhounding. Figures A and B identify some of the equipment you may be told you need at a site. Figure C shows material needed to collect, package, transport, and record your findings. Figure D illustrates typical safety equipment.

Always use safety glasses with side shields or goggles when you are hammering or chiseling. Chips of rock or metal from your tools can fly off at great speed in any direction when hammering. Use gloves to protect your hands as well.

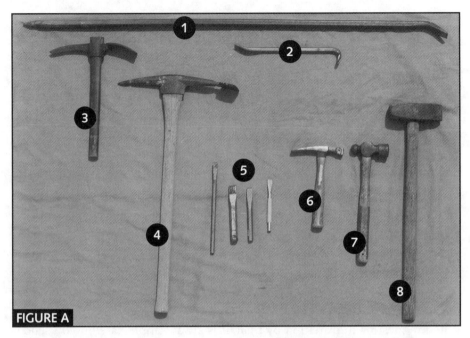

FIGURE A

1. Crowbar.
2. Pry bar.
3. Smaller pick.
4. Rock pick.
5. Various-sized chisels. (*Note:* When working with a hammer and chisel, you may want to use a chisel holder, not shown, for protecting your hand if you miss. Always use eye protection with side shields and gloves!)
6. Rock hammer. (*Note:* Always use eye protection.)
7. 3-pound hammer. (*Note:* Always use eye protection.)
8. Sledge hammer. (*Note:* When working with a sledge hammer, wear hard-toed boots along with eye protection.)

Other useful tools not shown include an ultraviolet hand lamp, and a hand magnifier.

Not pictured, but something you don't want to forget, is your camera and plenty of extra film. You may also want to bring along your video camera to record that "big" find, no matter what it might be.

Not pictured, but to be considered: knee pad and seat cushion.

Other Safety Precautions

- Never go into the field or on an unsupervised site alone. With protective clothing, reasonable care, proper use of equipment, and common sense,

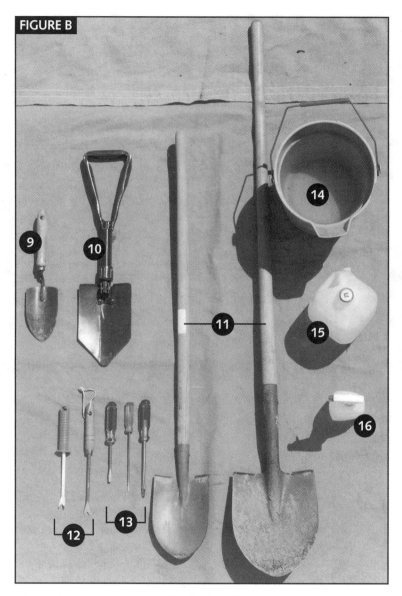

FIGURE B

9. Garden trowel.
10. Camp shovel.
11. Shovels.
12. Garden cultivators.
13. Screwdrivers.

14. Bucket of water.
15. (Plastic) jug of water.
16. Squirt bottle of water; comes in handy at many of the mines to wash off rocks so you can see if they are or contain gem material.

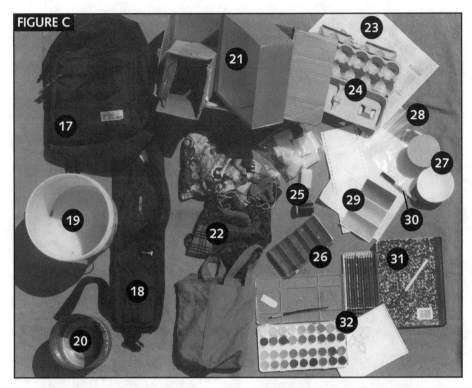

FIGURE C

17. Backpack.
18. Waist pack to hold specimens.
19. Bucket to hold specimens.
20. Coffee can to hold specimens.
21. Boxes to pack, transport, and ship specimens.
22. Bags—various sized bags to carry collected specimens in the field.
23. Newspaper to wrap specimens for transport.
24. Egg cartons to transport delicate specimens.
25. Empty film canisters to hold small specimens.
26. Plastic box with dividers to hold small specimens.
27. Margarine containers to hold small specimens.

28. Reclosable plastic bags to hold small specimens.
29. Gummed labels to label specimens. Whether you are at a fee dig site or with a guide, usually there will be someone to help you identify your find. It is a good idea to label the find when it is identified so that when you reach home, you won't have boxes of unknown rocks.
30. Waterproof marker for labeling.
31. Field log book to make notes on where specimens were found.
32. Sketching pencils, sketchbook, paint to record your finds and the surrounding scenery.

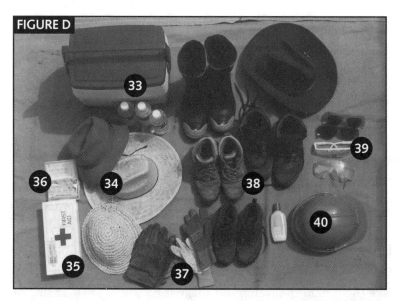

FIGURE D

33. Food and water—always carry plenty of drinking water. (*Note:* many sites tell you in advance if they have food and water available or if you should bring some; however, it is always a good idea to bring extra drinking water. Remember—if you bring it in, pack it back out.)

34. Hats. Many of the sites are in the open, and the summer sun can be hot and dangerous to unprotected skin. Check with the site to see if they have any recommendations for protective clothing. Also, don't forget sunscreen.

35. First aid/safety kit.

36. Snakebite kit. If the area is known to have snakes, be alert and take appropriate safety measures, such as boots and long pants. (*Note:* while planning our first gem-hunting trip, we read that the first aid kit should contain a snakebite kit. Just like rockhounds, snakes seem to love rocky areas!) In most cases, if you visit sites in the book, you will be either at a flume provided by the facility, or with an experienced guide. At the first, you will most likely never see a snake; at the second, your guide will fill you in on precautions. For listings where you will be searching on a ranch or state park, ask about special safety concerns such as snakes and insects when you pay your fee. These sites may not be for everyone.

37. Gloves to protect your hands when you are working with sharp rock or using a hammer or chisel.

38. Boots—particularly important at sites where you will be doing a lot of walking, or walking on rocks.

39. Safety glasses with side shields, or goggles. Particularly important at hard rock sites or any site where you or others may be hitting rocks. Safety glasses are available with tinted lenses for protection from the sun.

40. Hard hats—may be mandatory if you are visiting an active quarry or mine; suggested near cliffs.

accidents should be avoided, but in the event of an illness or accident, you always want to have someone with you who can administer first aid and call for or seek help.

- Always keep children under your supervision.
- Never enter old abandoned mines or underground diggings!
- Never break or hammer rocks close to another person!

Mining Techniques

How to Sluice for Gems

This is the most common technique used at fee dig mines where you buy a bucket of gem ore (gem dirt) and wash it at a flume.

1. Place a quantity of the gem ore in the screen box, and place the screen box in the water. Use enough gem ore to fill the box about a third.

2. Place the box in the water, and shake it back and forth, raising one side,

Clockwise from top: Gold pan; screen box used for sluicing; screen box used for screening.

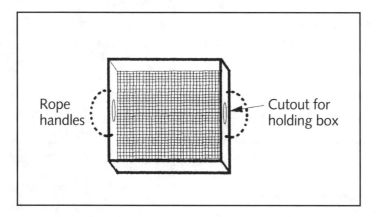

Rope handles

Cutout for holding box

How to Build a Screen Box

1. A screen box that is easy to handle is generally built from 1" x 4" lumber and window screening.

2. Decide on the dimensions of the screen box you want, and cut the wood accordingly. Dimensions generally run from 12" x 12" up to 18" x 18". Remember that the end pieces will overlap the side pieces, so cut the end pieces 1½" longer.

3. There are two alternative methods of construction. In one, drill pilot holes in the end pieces, and use wood screws to fasten the end pieces to the side pieces. In the other, use angle irons and screws to attach the ends and sides.

4. Cut the screening to be ¼" smaller than the outside dimensions of the screen box, and use staples to attach the screen to the bottom of the box. Use metal screening rather than plastic if possible. For a stronger box, cut ¼" or ⅜" hardware cloth to the same dimensions as the screening, and staple the hardware cloth over the screening. The hardware cloth will provide support for the screening.

5. Cut ¼" wood trim to fit, and attach it to the bottom of the box to cover the edges of the screening and hardware cloth and staples.

6. If you like, add rope handles or cut handholds in the side pieces for easier handling.

then the other, so that the material in the box moves back and forth. What you are doing is making the stones move around in the screen box, while washing dirt and sand out of the mixture.

3. After a minute or two of washing, take the screen box out of the flume, and let it drain. Look through the stones remaining in the screen box for your treasure. If you're not sure about something, ask one of the attendants.

4. When you can't finding anything more, put the box back in the flume and wash it some more, then take it out and search again.

5. If possible, move your screen box into bright light while you are searching, since the gems and minerals often show up better in bright light.

How to Screen for Gems

This is another common technique used at fee dig mines where you buy a bucket of gem ore and screen it for gems. (The authors used this technique for garnets and sapphires in Montana.)

1. Place a quantity of the gem ore in the screen box, and place the screen box in the water. Use enough gem dirt to fill the box about a third.

2. Place the box in the water, and begin tipping it back and forth, raising one side, then the other, so that the material in the box moves back and forth. What you are doing is making the gemstones, which are heavier than the rock and dirt, move into the bottom center of the screen box while at the same time washing dirt and sand out of the mixture.

3. After a minute or two, change the direction of movement to front and back.

4. Repeat these two movements (Steps 2 and 3) three or four times.

5. Take the box out of the water and let it drain, then place a board on top

and carefully flip the box over onto the sorting table. If you have done it right, the gemstones will be found in the center of the rocks dumped onto the board. Use tweezers to pick the rough gemstones out of the rocks, and place them in a small container.

How to Pan for Gold

The technique for panning for gold is based on the fact that gold is much heavier than rock or soil. Gently washing and swirling the gold-bearing soil in a pan causes the gold to settle to the bottom of the pan. A gold pan has a flat bottom and gently slanting sides. Some modern pans also have small ridges or rings around the inside of the pan on these slanting sides. As the soil is washed out of the pan, the gold will slide down the sides, or be caught on the ridges and stay in the pan. Here's how:

1. Begin by filling the pan with ore, about ⅔ to ¾ full.

2. Put your pan in the water, let it gently fill with water, then put the pan under the water surface. Leave the pan in the water, and mix the dirt around in the pan, cleaning and removing any large rocks.

3. Lift the pan out of the water, then gently shake the pan from side to side while swirling it at the same time. Do this for 20–30 seconds to get the gold settled to the bottom of the pan.

4. Still holding the pan out of the water, continue these motions while tilting the pan so that the dirt begins to wash out. Keep the angle of the pan so that the crease (where the bottom and sides meet) is the lowest point.

5. When there is only about a tablespoon of material left in the pan, put about ½ inch of water in the pan, and swirl the water over the remaining material. As the top material is moved off, you should see gold underneath.

6. No luck? Try again at a different spot.

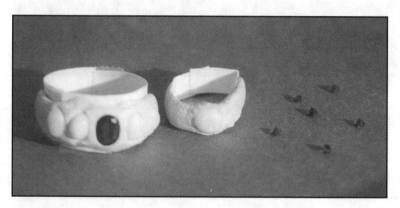

The authors sent their rough gems away for faceting. Using the faceted gems, they made crude mock-ups and sketches of the rings they wanted; then they sent the mock-ups, sketches, and gems to be made into rings.

The finished rings.

Notes on Gem Faceting, Cabbing, and Mounting Services

Many of the fee dig sites offer services to cut and mount your finds. Quality and costs vary. Trade journals such as *Lapidary Journal* and *Rock & Gem* (available at most large bookstores or by subscription) list suppliers of these services, both in the United States and overseas. Again, quality and cost vary. Local rock and gem shops in your area may offer these services, or it may be possible to work with a local jeweler. Finally, your local rock club may be able to provide these services or make recommendations.

After their first gem-hunting trip, the authors had some of their finds faceted and cabochoned. They then designed rings and had them made using these stones, as shown in the photos on the previous page.

Taking sifted gravel to the jig at a sapphire mine in Montana

ALABAMA

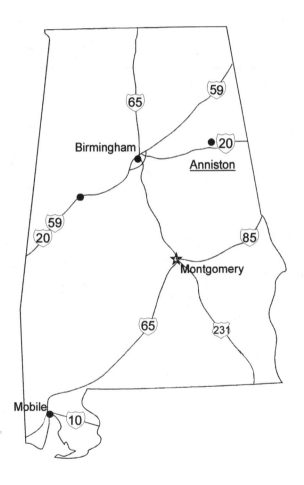

State Gemstone: Star Blue Quartz (1990)
State Mineral: Hematite (1967)
State Stone/Rock: Marble (1969)

SECTION 1: Fee Dig Sites and Guide Services

No information available.

SECTION 2: Museums and Mine Tours

ANNISTON

Museum 🏛

Anniston Museum of Natural History
P.O. Box 1587
800 Museum Drive
Anniston, AL 36202-1587
Phone: (256) 237-6766
Fax: (256) 237-6776
www.annistonmuseum.org

Open: Tuesday–Saturday 10:00 A.M.–5:00 P.M., Sunday 1:00–5:00 P.M., closed most Mondays.

Info: The Dynamic Earth exhibit details the processes and products of the formation of the earth as it traces the history of our ever-changing planet. Included in the exhibit are gemstones and a meteorite. The Underground World exhibit contains one of only a few man-made indoor caves in the Southeast.

Admission: Adults $3.50, children 4–17 $2.50, discounts for seniors.

Directions: Anniston, in Calhoun County, is 60 miles northeast of Birmingham and 80 miles west of Atlanta, GA. It is easily accessible by I-20, U.S. 21, and U.S. 431.

SECTION 3: Special Events and Tourist Information

TOURIST INFORMATION

State Tourist Agency

Alabama Bureau of Tourism
401 Adams Avenue
P.O. Box 4927
Montgomery, AL 36103-4927
Phone: (800) ALABAMA or
(800) 252-2262
www.touralabama.org

Quartz Crystals

Although quartz makes up nearly 25% of the earth's surface, only three known places have enough high-quality crystal to warrant commercial mining. These are Brazil, Madagascar (a small island off the coast of Africa), and the Ouachita Mountain range of Arkansas. Quartz is the leading mineral mined in the Ouachita Mountains, which rank among the oldest mountain ranges in the U.S. Quartz is found in open crystal pockets formed in the sandstone, shale, and other rocks of the region. Crystals were once dug by Native Americans, who may have used and traded the crystals for religious and medicinal purposes.

Quartz crystals formed of silicon and oxygen are hexagonal structures that have the unique property of piezoelectricity, which means that they respond in a direct vibratory pattern when stimulated electrically or by pressure. Because of its piezoelectric qualities, quartz crystal can be used to amplify, transform, focus, and transfer energy. During World War II, quartz from Fisher Mountain was used by the U.S. Government for oscillators in radios.

There are several types of crystals, including single and double terminated, small to large clusters, and tabulars. Although a crystal can shatter, it is hard enough to cut glass (on the Mohs hardness scale a crystal is rated 7; a diamond 10). It is considered a semiprecious stone and is valuable to those who invest in and collect minerals.

Crystals are used in several fields, including industry, jewelry, and electronics. The piezoelectricity property makes quartz crystals indispensable to the international electronics industry for use in everything from radios and watches to Silicon Valley microcomputer chips, and thousands of products in between.

The use of quartz crystals in the metaphysical field to amplify, transform, focus, and transfer energy has led to a growing interest in them by groups and individuals who use the clear crystals for purposes generally described as healing. Quartz crystals are said to be dedicated healers that balance all elements needed to make a person whole. Quartz is claimed to be a purifier, which creates harmony and balance.

You can dig these quartz crystals in several mines located in the Mt. Ida area.

ARKANSAS

State Gemstone: Diamond
State Mineral: Quartz
State Stone/Rock: Bauxite

GLENWOOD / *Native · Moderate*

Dig Your Own Quartz Crystals *T*

The following gems or minerals may be found:

▪ Quartz crystals

Crystal Hills Mining Company
Tim Hill
Route 1, Box 926
Glenwood, AR 71943
Phone: (870) 356-4615
www.eyesoftime.com/hillmine

Open: By appointment only
Info: This is a working mine. Dig in the walls and veins, or simply pick up crystals from the tailings (material left over during mining operations). Mine personnel will show you where to find crystals. This is a primitive area with no facilities, services, or phones. Bring your own equipment and containers. Stay away from flagged areas and from machinery.
Admission: Adults $20.00, keep all you find.
Directions: Turn south off State Highway 27 onto Logan Gap Road. Drive approximately 2.6 miles, then turn right at crossroads 177. Follow the signs toward Collier Springs. Proceed 1 mile to the concrete low-water bridge. The mine entrance is approximately 100 feet past the bridge on the left.

HOT SPRINGS / *Native · Moderate*

Dig Your Own Quartz Crystals *T*

The following gems or minerals may be found:

▪ Quartz crystals

Coleman's Crystal Mine
Ron Coleman Mining, Inc.
P.O. Box 8219
Hot Springs, AR 71910
Phone: (501) 984-5396; (800) 291-4484
Fax: (501) 984-5443
E-mail: colemans@cswnet.com
www.omtp.com/colemans

Open: Year round, 7 days/week. Winter, 8:00 A.M.–4:30 P.M. Summer, 8:00 A.M.–5:30 P.M.
Info: This is a working mine. Crystal digging is in 40 acres of mine tailings (material left over during mining operations) with fresh material routinely excavated, weather permitting. Keep all you find. Equipment is provided, including crystal washing stations.
Admission: Adults $20.00, students (7–16) $5.00, children under 7 free.
Other services available: Retail shop, wholesale showroom for dealers, snack shop, gift shop. Coleman's Rocks-R-Gems retail store is located at 1700 East Grand in Hot Springs National Park at the intersection of Highway 70 east and

Digging Quartz

Bring a suitable digging tool such as a rock hammer, screwdriver, shovel, trowel, or anything to scratch around with. Wear old clothes, since the red clay stains anything it comes in contact with. On sunny days, a hat and sunscreen are suggested, along with drinking water. Hand tools are recommended to preserve the crystallography of the specimens.

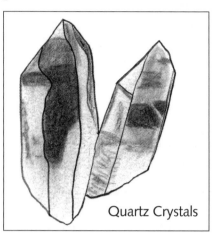

Quartz Crystals

Cleaning Quartz

One process for cleaning quartz is to soak the crystals in a mild solution of oxalic acid. Use 1 pound of oxalic acid to 2½ gallons water. The cleaning procedure should be carried out only by an adult. Dissolve the oxalic acid in warm water in any container except aluminum. Soak crystals 4 to 5 days. Keep the solution properly labeled and in a secure place covered from the sun when in use or not. The solution can be reused up to three times. Be sure to follow the safety instructions when working with oxalic acid.

(Information provided by Sonny Stanley's Mine)

70B, open 8:00 A.M.–5:00 P.M. daily.

Campground: Crystal Ridge RV Park (located on the grounds of Ron Coleman Mining, Inc.) has 26 quiet, shady sites on a paved circle. Services offered: modern restrooms, clean hot showers, washateria, dump station, water and electric hookups.

Directions: The mine is located on Little Blakeley Road 1½ mile from Highway 7N, 14 miles north of Hot Springs.

MOUNT IDA / *Native • Moderate*

Dig Your Own
Quartz Crystals T

The following gems or minerals may be found:

▪ Quartz crystals

Crystal Heaven
401 Sunrise Hills Drive
Mount Ida, AR 71957
Phone: (870) 867-4625

Open: May 1–Thanksgiving, 8:30 A.M.–3:00 P.M., 7 days/week.
Admission: $20.00. Dig your own—keep all that you find.
Directions: Located 4 miles east of Mt. Ida on Sunrise Hills Drive.

MOUNT IDA / *Native • Moderate*

Dig Your Own
Quartz Crystals T

The following gems or minerals may be found:

▪ Quartz crystals

Crystal Pyramid
HC 63, Box 136A
Mount Ida, AR 71957
Phone: (870) 867-2568

Open: Monday–Saturday 9:00 A.M.–5:00 P.M., Sunday 1:00–5:00 P.M.
Admission:
▪ Option 1, Paid admission, $10.00/person 13 and older, $5.00/person under 13 years old.
▪ Option 2, make purchases at the store above the minimum amount for admission to the mine, $20.00 merchandise/person 13 and older, $10.00 merchandise/person under 13 years old.
Other services available: Store.
Directions: Pick up a map and get verbal directions to the mine at the store when you pay for digging. The store is located on Route 270, 4 miles east of Mt. Ida.

MOUNT IDA / *Native • Moderate*

Dig Your Own
Quartz Crystals T

The following gems or minerals may be found:

▪ Quartz crystals

Fiddler's Ridge Rock Shop & Crystal Mines
Jim and Kathy Fecho
HC 63, Box 211J
Mount Ida, AR 71957
Phone: (870) 867-2127

Open: Year round, 9:00 A.M.–5:00 P.M., 7 days/week.
Admission: Adults $10.00/day, children 6–12 $5.00, children under 6 free.
Other services available: Gift shop.
Directions: Located 7 miles east of Mt. Ida on U.S. 270.

MOUNT IDA / *Native* • *Moderate*

Dig Your Own Quartz Crystals 𝓣

The following gems or minerals may be found:

• Quartz crystals

Leatherhead Quartz Mining
Tony and Terri Thacker
HC 67, Box 62P
Pencil Bluff, AR 71965
(Mine located in Mount Ida)
Phone: (870) 326-4871
Fax: (870) 326-4680
E-mail: LTHERHEAD@aol.com

Open: Call ahead; appointment required. 9:00 A.M.–5:00 P.M., 7 days/week, weather permitting.
Info: Three acres of open pit are available for digging. Keep all you find; no weight limits.
Admission: Adults: 20.00/day or $5.00/hour, children under 11 and adults 80 and older free.
Directions: Take U.S. 270 to Mt. Ida. Turn onto Route 27 south between the

Exxon and the Total gas stations. Travel approximately 3½ miles, then turn left on Owley Road (first paved road outside Mt. Ida city limits). Continue past end of pavement, crossing three small bridges. Turn right at the sign at the top of the hill.

MOUNT IDA / *Native* • *Moderate*

Dig Your Own Quartz Crystals 𝓣

The following gems or minerals may be found:

• Quartz crystals

Robins Mining Company
Mearl and Lorraine Robins
P.O. Box 236
Mount Ida, AR 71957
Phone: (870) 867-2530
Fax: (870) 867-4672

Open: Year round, Monday–Friday 8:00 A.M.–5:00 P.M. Can make arrangements in advance to dig on weekends.
Admission: $10.00/day per person; keep all you find. Children under 8 dig free.
Info: Stop at Crystal House to pay fee, sign a liability waiver, and get a pass and map to the mine. Digging at the mine is for recreational purposes only. Only hand tools are allowed—bring your own.
Other services available: Rock shop—variety of quality quartz and other minerals.

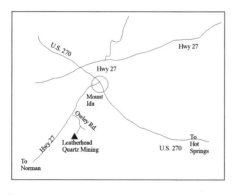

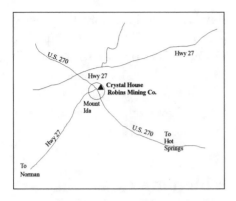

Directions: The Crystal House Shop is located at the intersection of Highway 270 and 27 South. The mine is located nearby.

Native • Moderate

Dig Your Own Quartz Crystals—Open Pit Mining *T*

The following gems or minerals may be found:

- Quartz crystals

Sonny Stanley's Crystal Mine
P.O. Box 163
Mount Ida, AR 71957
Phone: (870) 867-3556 (day);
(870) 867-3719 (night)

Open: Year round, 7 days/week. 8:30 A.M.–5:00 P.M. Longer summer hours.

Admission: Free. If specimens are collected, a donation is requested to offset overhead expenses. A key for access to the prospecting area may be obtained with a donation at the "rock yard."

Group reservations requested, especially during tourist season.

Other services available: Rock shop with over 300 types of minerals, museum. On-site accommodations are limited to parking space for self-contained campers.

Directions: The rock shop and museum are located on Pine Street off Highway 270. The mine is located approximately 10 miles from the rock shop.

Native • Moderate

Dig Your Own Quartz Crystals *T*

The following gems or minerals may be found:

- Quartz crystals

Starfire Mine
Charlie and Chris Burch
HC 63, Box 306
Mount Ida, AR 71957
Phone: (870) 867-2431
Fax: (870) 867-0159
E-mail: crystals@ipa.net
www.starfirecrystals.com

Open: Year round, 6:30 A.M.–8:00 P.M., summer until 10:00 P.M., 7 days/week.

Admission: $20.00/day, children under 12 free. Tools may be rented for $10.00/day.

Other services available: Two rock shops, larger one open by appointment; snack shop; motel.

Directions: Located 12 miles east of Mt. Ida on U.S. 270.

MOUNT IDA / *Native—Enriched* · *Easy to Moderate*

Dig Your Own Quartz Crystals or Pan for Gemstones T

The following gems or minerals may be found:

- Quartz crystals; also rubies, emeralds, amethysts, and more

Wegner Crystal Mines
Richard Wegner
P.O. Box 205
Mount Ida, AR 71957
Phone: (870) 867-2309

Open: Year round, 8:00 A.M.–5:00 P.M., 7 days/week. Reservations required.

Info: Dig quartz crystals at one of three operating mines, or sluice for gemstones at a salted mine at a shaded lakeside location. Quartz crystals may be dug at one of three mines. Two of them, the world-famous Phantom Mine and the Crystal Mine, are located between 20 and 30 minutes' drive from the Visitors Center; transportation is provided to and from these mines. The first trip leaves at 8:45 A.M., and the last trip departs at 1:30 P.M., to allow for 4 full hours of digging. The third mine, the Old Mountaintop Mine, is located a ¼-mile strenuous climb from the visitors center. You may dig all day for one fee.

The salted mine is located adjacent to the campground.

Admission:
- Phantom Mine $20.00/person, $40.00 minimum required per trip.
- Crystal Mine $15.00/person, $30.00 minimum required per trip.
- Old Mountain Top $12.00/person.
- Children under 12 half price on the above prices.

   Free tool and bucket with every admission.
- Salted mine, easy for children and seniors, $6.00/adult; dig all day.
- Children under 12 half price.
- Sluice mine $5.00/adult, $2.50/child under 12.
- Gemstone bags with rubies, emeralds, and more, $1.25/bag. Bags with crystal "diamonds," amethysts, and more, $0.75/bag.

Other services available: Rock shop with a variety of quartz quality and of other minerals, famous 10,000 square foot wholesale barn, snack shop, tour showing the process of preparing quartz for shipment worldwide.

Campground: $7.00 per tent, $9.00 per vehicle with electric hookup, $2.00 extra for air conditioning or portable heaters.

   Services offered: Shady sites, modern restrooms, clean hot showers, fishing, swimming hole, dump station, activities for children, firewood.

Directions: Located 8 miles south of Mt. Ida, off Owley Road, which comes

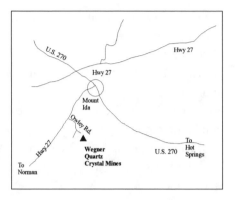

off Highway 27. Take Route 27 south from Mount Ida. Travel approximately 3½ miles, then turn left on Owley Road (first paved road outside Mt. Ida city limits). Follow Owley Road to the mine.

MURFREESBORO / *Native* ▪ *Moderate*

Dig Your Own Diamonds and Other Gems 𝑇

The following gems or minerals may be found:

▪ Diamonds are the chief attraction; however, amethyst, agate, jasper, quartz, calcite, barite, peridot, and up to 40 other gems or minerals can also be found.

Crater of Diamonds State Park
Route 1, Box 364
Murfreesboro, AR 71958
Phone: (870) 285-3113

Open: Year round except major holidays. December–February 8 A.M.–4:30 P.M., May 21–September 5 8:00 A.M.–8 P.M., rest of the year 8:00 A.M.–5:00 P.M. **Info:** Crater of Diamonds State Park offers a one-of-a-kind adventure—the chance to find and keep real diamonds. You can search a 36½-acre field of lamproite soil, which is the eroded surface of an ancient gem-bearing volcanic pipe (lava tube). Prospectors enter the field through a visitors center that includes exhibits and an audiovisual program explaining the area's geology and providing tips on recognizing diamonds in the rough.

Since diamonds were first discovered there in 1906, more than 70,000 have been found. Since the crater became a state park in 1972, over 19,000 diamonds have been found by visitors, and on the average, more than 600 diamonds are found each year. Among the diamonds that have been found are the Uncle Sam (40.23 carats), the Star of Murfreesboro (34.2 carats), the Star of Arkansas (15.33 carats), and the Amarillo Starlight (16.37 carats).

The park consists of 888 pine-covered acres along the banks of the Little Missouri River. The first diamond was found in 1906; the property has changed hands several times over the years. Previous owners made several attempts to mine diamonds commercially. These attempts are mostly shrouded in mystery, and all ultimately failed; lawsuits, fires, or lack of capital are some of the reasons for failure. In 1972, the

State of Arkansas bought the property and established Crater of Diamonds State Park.

Lamproite, a relatively rare rock of magmatic origin, is a source rock containing commercially viable concentrations of diamonds. The lamproite soil, very different from red Arkansas clay, is dark green to black, gummy when wet, and powdery when dry. Wyoming and Colorado have several diamond deposits similar to those at Crater of Diamonds State Park and also similar to those mined in South Africa.

This is the only diamond field open to the public in North America. The field is plowed approximately monthly. The park staff at the visitors center will aid you in the identification of any stone you find.

Diamond mining tools, such as army shovels, trowels, gardening tools, and screen boxes, can be rented or purchased at the park. Two mineral-washing pavilions contain huge dumpsters filled with water to aid in screening for diamonds.

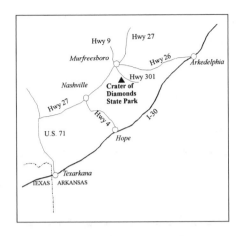

Any organized group may dig at one half the regular fee. Advance notice must be given to obtain the reduced rate.

The State Park offers a variety of orientation programs during the summer months: programs cover nature, geology, diamond-"hunting" methods, and history. **Admission:** Adults $4.50, children (6–12) $2.00, children under 6 free. Between Memorial Day and Labor Day, admission tickets purchased after 6:00 P.M. are good for the following day.

Other services available: Restaurant (seasonal), gift shop, restrooms, river

Diamond-Hunting Tips

Look for small, well-rounded crystals. A diamond weighing several carats may be no larger than a marble. Look for clean crystals, since diamonds have an oily, slick outer surface that dirt and mud don't stick to. The diamonds come in several colors. The most common found at the crater are clear white, yellow, and brown.

trail, interpretive exhibits, historical structures, fishing.

A 1.3-mile-long river trail winds its way through the woods to the scenic Little Missouri River. This provides a relaxing 1-hour hike over level terrain.

Campground: 60 Class A campsites in a secluded woodsview setting. Water and electric hookups are available.

Services offered: Shady sites, modern restrooms, clean hot showers, laundry facilities, dump station, tent sites, nearby fishing.

Directions: The State Park is located 2 miles southeast from Murfreesboro on Arkansas Route 301.

SECTION 2: Museums and Mine Tours

FAYETTEVILLE

Museum 🏛

The University Museum
The Museum Building
The University of Arkansas
Fayetteville, AR 72701
Phone: (501) 575-3466; (501) 575-8766

Open: All year, Monday–Saturday 9:00 A.M.–4:30 P.M.

Info: Exhibits on rocks and minerals include geology of the Fayetteville area, Arkansas' mineral wealth, and quartz of Arkansas.

Admission: Adults $2.00, children $1.00.

Directions: On Garland Avenue (Highway 112) at the intersection with Maple Avenue.

LITTLE ROCK

Museum 🏛

Geology Learning Center
Arkansas Geological Commission
3815 W. Roosevelt Road
Little Rock, AR 72204
Phone: (501) 296-1877; (501) 663-9714

Open: All year between 8:00 A.M. and 4:30 P.M., by appointment only. Call one of the geologists at the Commission to make an appointment.

Info: The learning center is intended to give students of all ages who are interested in earth sciences direct exposure to rocks, minerals, fossils and fuels. Exhibits include the Arkansas Geological Commission, Arkansas' mineral wealth, fossil fuels in Arkansas, Arkansas

gems and minerals, and Arkansas fossils.
Admission: Free.
Directions: Located at 1911 Thayer Street, just south of the intersection of West Asher and West Wright Avenues.

STATE UNIVERSITY

Museum

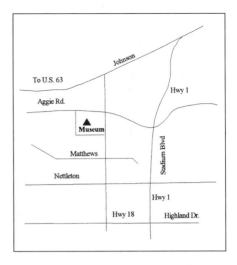

ASU Museum
Arkansas State University
Museum/Library Building
P.O. Box 490
State University, AR 72467
Phone: (501) 972-2074

Open: All year, closed campus holidays. Monday–Friday 9:00 A.M.–4:00 P.M., Saturday and Sunday 1:00–4:00 P.M.
Info: Exhibits include a chart showing relative lengths of the periods of the earth's formation, several fossils, and a variety of minerals, including a large number found in Arkansas. Arkansas minerals displayed include fluorite, bauxite, calcite clusters, halite, granite, gypsum, quartz and drusy quartz, smithsonite, golden dolomite and dolomite crystals, selenite, nepheline syenite and septarian concretions.
Admission: Free, donations appreciated.
Directions: ASU is on the eastern outskirts of Jonesboro.

ANNUAL EVENT

Quartz Crystal Festival and World Championship Dig, Mount Ida 🐾

In Mount Ida (Quartz Crystal Capital of the World), dig in actual working quartz crystal mines in the heart of the Ouachita Mountains. The contest is held as part of the Annual Quartz, Quiltz, and Craftz Festival. The festival includes a gem and mineral show and is held on the second Friday, Saturday, and Sunday in October.

The dig begins on Thursday, one day before the Festival. Diggers have three days to dig. The hours are 9:00 A.M. to 3:00 P.M. Prize money is awarded to the top five winners in each division; crystal trophies go to the first- and second-place winners in each division.

Registration fee: $60.00/person before September 15, $75.00/person after September 15, $40.00 each for a group of 30 or more.

Prizes, costs, and deadlines change from year-to-year, so call for details. Keep all you dig; use hand tools only (provide your own). Ages 10–16 permitted to dig with adult supervision. Primitive toilets are available at dig sites. At the festival, crystals, gems, minerals, jewelry, equipment, supplies, books, dealers, and exhibits are available. For further details and a registration form, write to:

Mt. Ida Chamber of Commerce
P.O. Box 6
Highway 270 and Elder Street
Mt. Ida, AR 71957
Phone: (870) 867-2723
E-mail: mountida@ipa.net
www.mtidachamber.com

The Chamber of Commerce can also provide information on the Ouachita National Forest, the South's oldest and largest national forest, covering 1.6 million acres. Features include Lake Ouachita, which offers fishing, scuba diving, water skiing, sailing, horseback riding, camping, and hiking; 480 miles of hiking trails run throughout the National Forest.

TOURIST INFORMATION

State Tourist Agency 🐾

Arkansas Department of Parks and Tourism
One Capital Mall
Little Rock, AR 72201
Phone: (501) 682-7772;
(800) NATURAL or (800) 628-8725
Fax: (501) 682-1364
E-mail: arkansas@1800natural.com
www.1800natural.com

Mt. Ida Area Chamber of Commerce
P.O. Box 6
Mt. Ida, AR 71957
Phone: (870) 867-2723
E-mail: mountida@ipa.net
www.mtidachamber.com

Hot Springs Convention and Visitors Bureau
P.O. Box K
Hot Springs National Park, AR 71902-1982
Phone: (800) SPA-CITY or (800) 772-2489
www.hotsprings.org

FLORIDA

State Gemstone: Moonstone
State Stone/Rock: Agatized coral

SECTION 1: Fee Dig Sites and Guide Services

No information available.

SECTION 2: Museums and Mine Tours

MULBERRY

Museum 🏛

Mulberry Phosphate Museum
P.O. Box 707
Mulberry, FL 33860
Phone: (941) 425-2823

Open: All year, Tuesday–Saturday 10:00 A.M.–4:30 P.M. Special tours can be arranged by calling.
Info: The museum houses educational exhibits on the phosphate industry.

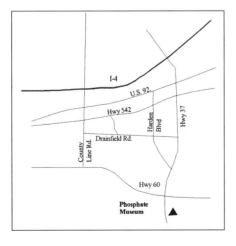

Admission: Donation requested.
Directions: One block south of State Highway 60 on State Highway 37 in downtown Mulberry.
Note: The phosphate deposits are rich in fossils. Please see our sequel directory to fossil sites.

TAMPA

Museum 🏛

Ed and Bernadette Marcin Museum,
Department of Geology
University of South Florida
East Fowler Avenue, Room 534
Tampa, FL 33620
Phone: (813) 974-2236

Open: All year by appointment only, Monday–Friday except holidays. Special arrangements can be made for groups.
Info: Located in Room 534 of the Science Center at the University of South Florida's Tampa Campus. This is a small museum, which includes minerals and

gemstones created through the donations of Dr. and Mrs. Pious. They accumulated their collection over a period of about 20 years, largely while traveling through the western U.S. and Florida. The museum collection is augmented and maintained through gifts to the departmental collection and by collectors throughout Florida. Included in the museum collections are an agatized wood collection and a mineral collection.

Admission: Free.

Directions: The museum is located in the Science Center at the University of South Florida–Tampa campus.

SECTION 3: Special Events and Tourist Information

TOURIST INFORMATION

State Tourist Agency

Florida Division of Tourism
126 Van Buren St.
Tallahassee, FL 32301
Phone: (904) 487-1462 or
(904) 487 1463
www.see-florida.com

GEORGIA

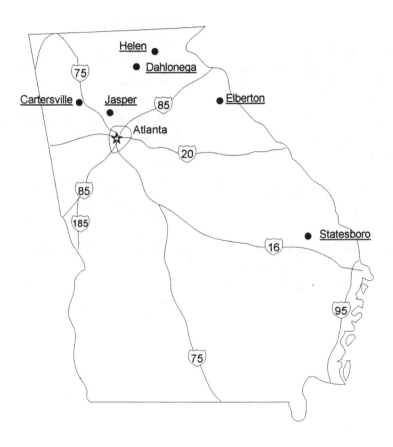

State Gemstone: Quartz
State Mineral: Staurolite

DAHLONEGA / *Easy*

Pan for Gold *T*

*The following gems or minerals
may be found:*

▪ Gold

Consolidated Gold Mine
185 Consolidated Gold Mine Road
Dahlonega, GA 30533
Phone: (706) 864-8473

Open: All year, 7 days/week. Winter,
10:00 A.M.–4:00 P.M. Summer, 10:00
A.M.–5:00 P.M.

Info: For further information on the
Consolidated Gold Mine tour, see Section 2.

Rates: Panning is included in the mine
tour fee, or alone at $3.00/person.

Other services available: Mine tour,
shops.

Directions: ¾ mile east of Dahlonega
on Highway 52, where Highways 52,
60, 19, and 9 merge.

DAHLONEGA / *Easy*

Pan for Gold or Gemstones *T*

*The following gems or minerals
may be found:*

▪ **Gold, rubies, emeralds, garnets, sapphires, and many more**

Crisson Gold Mine
2736 Morrison Moore Parkway East
Dahlonega, GA 30533
Phone: (706) 864-6363

Open: All year, 10:00 A.M.–6:00 P.M.
April–October, 10:00 A.M.–5:00 P.M.
November–March, 7 days/week.

Info: The mine offers indoor panning in

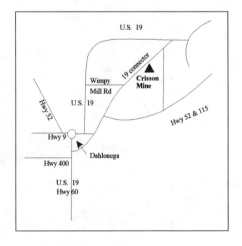

Dahlonega: Site of America's First Gold Rush

DAH-LON-E-GA is the word in the Cherokee language for the "precious yellow metal" found in these hills. In 1828, the cry "We've found gold" was heard far and near. With the discovery of gold in the foothills of the Blue Ridge Mountains, Dahlonega emerged in 1833 as a full-blown "hustle and bustle" town. Gold was mined into the early 20th century. Now, several attractions highlight the town's historic activities, including a gold museum, gold panning, and gold mine tours. Attend Gold Rush Days, or come for the gold panning championships.

Information on the area may be obtained by contacting the Dahlonega-Lumpkin County Chamber of Commerce, Dahlonega, GA 30533, Phone: (706) 864-3711.

Elberton Granite

Elberton is hailed as the Granite Capital of the World. While most granite quarries are less than 150 feet deep, geologists estimate the Elberton deposit to be 2 to 3 miles in depth. The physical properties and characteristics are perfect for the over 200,000 granite monuments, markers, and mausoleums made in Elberton each year.

winter; ore is also sold "to go."

Rates: One pan of gold ore $2.00, 2½-gallon bucket of gold ore $5.75, 5-gallon bucket of gold ore $8.50, 2-gallon bucket of gem dirt $3.50, 5-gallon bucket of gem dirt $6.50.

Other services available: Tour and demonstration of a 113-year-old stamp mill, picnic area, gift shop, restrooms.

Directions: On U.S. 19 Connector, 2½ miles from downtown Dahlonega.

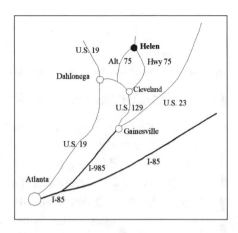

HELEN / *Easy*

Pan for Gold or Gemstones *T*

The following gems or minerals may be found:

• Gold, amethyst, citrine, garnet, topaz, smoky and rose quartz, and many more

Gold Mines of Helen, Georgia
Bruckenstr. 10
P.O. Box 278
Helen, Georgia 30545
Phone: (706) 878-3052

Open: Daily Memorial Day–Labor Day, weekends in spring (call), 10:00 A.M.–6:00 P.M.

Rates: Gold: pan $3.50; bucket: regular $7.50. Gems: small bucket $3.50; bucket: regular $7.50, extra large $15.00.

Other services available: Mine tour, restrooms, gift shops.

See listing in Section 2 for more details.

Directions: Helen is on State Highway 75, northeast of Atlanta.

World's Largest Open-Pit Marble Quarry

What is reported to be the world's largest open-pit marble quarry is located in Tate. A tract of land purchased in 1834 by Sam Tate was found to have a large deposit of marble. Mining began a few years later, and marble from this quarry has been used in building construction around the country. The Marble Festival is held in nearby Jasper, Georgia, every October; this is the only time when this quarry can be toured.

CARTERSVILLE

Museum 🏛

William Weinman Mineral Museum
51 Mineral Museum
Cartersville, GA 30120
Phone: (770) 386-0576
Fax: (770) 386-0600
E-mail: weinman51@aol.com

Open: All year, Tuesday–Saturday 10:00 A.M.–4:30 P.M., Sunday 1:00–4:30 P.M.
Info: In 1983, funds donated by the family of William J. Weinman, a pioneer in barite mining in Barstow County, were used to establish a museum in his honor. Frank Mayo, a prominent chemical manufacturer, added the Frank and Winnifred Mayo Wing and Library. The mission of the museum is to educate its visitors about the earth sciences, rocks, minerals, fossils, and gemstones.

Over 2,000 specimens are featured in three exhibit halls. The Georgia Room exhibits displays from the state and a simulated cave and waterfall. The Frank and Winnifred Mayo Wing contains international collections.
Admission: Adults $3.50, seniors $3.00, children (6–12) $2.50.
Other services available: The museum gift shop features mineral specimens, rock collections, gemstones, faceted jewelry, books, and educational kits. A mineral garden contains antique pieces of mining equipment and large mineral specimens.

The annual rock swap at the Weinman is held the 2nd Saturday in June, featuring special lectures and demonstrations, free admission to the museum, and dealers.
Directions: Exit 126 off I-75 and U.S. 441.

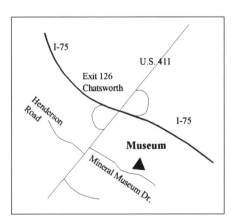

DAHLONEGA

Mine Tour 🏛

Consolidated Gold Mine
185 Consolidated Gold Mine Road
Dahlonega, GA 30533
Phone: (706) 864-8473

Open: All year, 7 days/week. Winter, 10:00 A.M.–4:00 P.M. Summer, 10:00 A.M.–5:00 P.M.

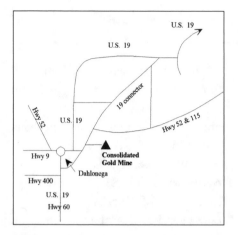

Info: Tour an actual underground gold mine as it appeared at the turn of the century. See displays of the actual equipment used, and discuss the excavating and mining techniques used. Learn the geology of the quartz and pyrite formations with which the early miners worked. Walk through the tunnel network complete with the original track system. The tour lasts 40 to 45 minutes. The mine is 60°F all year, so dress appropriately.

Admission: Adults $8.00, children (6–12) $5.00.

Other services available: Souvenir shop (offers a variety of rocks and minerals), restrooms.

Directions: ¾ mile east of Dahlonega on Highway 52, where Highways 52, 60, 19, and 9 merge.

DAHLONEGA

Museum, State Historic Site

Dahlonega Gold Museum
State Historic Site
Public Square
Dahlonega, GA 30533
Phone: (706) 864-2257

Open: Year round, 9:00 A.M.–5:00 P.M. Monday–Saturday, 10:00 A.M.–5:00 P.M. Sunday. Closed major holidays.

Info: The museum tells the story of the nation's first notable gold rush. In 1828, 20 years before the discovery of gold in California, thousands of gold seekers flocked to the area inhabited by the Cherokee Nation in north Georgia. They were drawn by the first major gold rush in the U.S. For more than 20 years prospectors continued to arrive, and the gold towns of Auroria and Dahlonega prospered. Between 1838 and 1861, more than $6 million in gold was coined

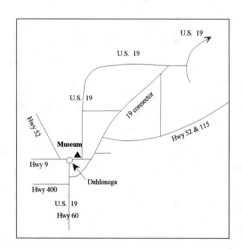

by the U.S. Branch Mint in Dahlonega.
Admission: Adults $2.50, children (6–18) $1.50. Group discounts.
Directions: Inside the city limits of Dahlonega, on the Public Square.

ELBERTON

Mine Tour 🏛

Elberton Granite Museum & Exhibit
Elberton Granite Association, Inc.
P.O. Box 640
Elberton, GA 30635
Phone: (706) 283-2551

Open: Daily January 15–November 15, 2:00–5:00 P.M. Closed Sunday. Limited schedule November 15–January 15; call for hours.
Info: The museum contains historical exhibits and artifacts, educational displays, and materials about the granite industry. Exhibit space on three levels graphically displays the unique granite products of the past, antique granite-working tools, and yesteryear's methods

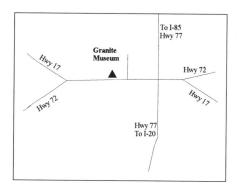

of quarrying, sawing, polishing, cutting, and sandblasting granite cemetery memorials. Exhibits also show how current quarrying methods and fabricating processes are carried out in Elberton's 35 different quarries and more than 100 manufacturing plants.
Admission: Free.
Directions: Elberton is located in northeast Georgia, midway between I-85 and I-20. From the north, take State Highway 17 south from the Lavonia Exit on I-85 until you come to the granite museum. From the south, take State Highway 77 from the Union Point exit on I-20, to Elberton, then turn left on Highway 17 to the museum, or from the Washington exit on I-20, take State Highway 17/U.S. 78 north and follow State Highway 17 to Elberton, to the museum.

HELEN

Mine Tour 🏛

Gold Mines of Helen, GA
Bruckenstr. 10
P.O. Box 278
Helen, GA 30545
Phone: (706) 878-3052

Open: Daily, June–August; weekends April–May, September–October, 10:00 A.M.–6:00 P.M.
Info: Tour the world-famous 300-foot-deep tunnel of the England Gold Mine.
Other features offered: Scenic nature trail to an ancient Indian dwelling cave;

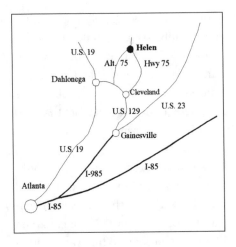

a display of unusual mining equipment; panning for gold or gemstones (see listing in Section 1).

Rates for mine tour: Adults $4.00, children $2.00. Group rates available.

Directions: Helen is on State Highway 75, northeast of Atlanta.

STATESBORO

Museum 🏛

Georgia Southern Museum
Landrum Box 8061
Rosenwald Building
Statesboro, GA 30460
Phone: (912) 681-5444; (912) 681-0147

Open: Year round; closed on major holidays. 9:00 A.M.–5:00 P.M. Monday–Friday, 10:00 A.M.–5:00 P.M. in summer, 2:00–5:00 P.M. Saturday–Sunday.

Info: The museum's Hall of Natural History contains a collection of rocks and minerals from Georgia's highland, piedmont, and coastal regions.

Admission: Free.

Directions: On the campus of Georgia Southern University.

SECTION 3: Special Events and Tourist Information

ANNUAL EVENT

Pickens County Marble Festival, Jasper, GA 🐎

First full weekend of October

For more information:
Pickens County Chamber of Commerce
500 Stegall Drive
Jasper, GA 30143

Phone: (706) 692-5600
Fax: 692-9453
E-mail: pickensc@nelson.tds.net
www.ngnet.com/pickensga

Info: Originally the Cherokee Indians' homeland, this part of north Georgia received its first white settlers in the 18th century. In 1834, Sam Tate purchased a large tract of land and opened

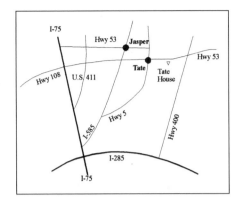

a tavern. An enormous vein of marble, 2,000 feet wide, 4 miles long, and up to ½ mile deep was soon discovered in the area owned by Sam Tate. Sam's son Stephen began the mining industry, which placed Tate on the map. Through his efforts the railroad was built through Pickens County, and Georgia marble was shipped throughout the country as construction material for many important buildings and monuments.

The Georgia Marble Company currently operates the world's largest open-pit marble quarry. It is open to the public by special tour only during the Marble Festival. Tours leave every 15 minutes from the festival grounds. Reservations are required.

Tour: Adults $7.00 plus festival admission $3.00, children $4.00, children under 4 free.

Other services available: Stephen Tate's son, Sam Tate, built a mansion in 1926 constructed of rare pink Etowah marble (the Tate House). This building has been renovated and is now a bed and breakfast. Tours of the mansion are available: (770) 735-3122.

Directions: Take I-575 to U.S. 515, which goes to the festival grounds.

TOURIST INFORMATION

State Tourist Agency

Georgia Department of Industry, Trade, and Tourism
P.O. Box 1776
Atlanta, GA 30301-1776
Phone: (404) 656-3590;
(800) VISIT-GA or (800) 847-4842
www.gomm.com
www.georgia.org

KENTUCKY

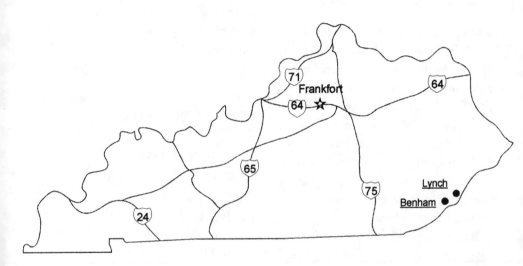

State Gemstone: Freshwater Pearl

SECTION 1: Fee Dig Sites and Guide Services

No information available.

SECTION 2: Museums and Mine Tours

BENHAM

Museum

Kentucky Coal Mine Museum
Tri-City Chamber of Commerce
Cumberland, KY 40823
Phone: (606) 848-1530
Fax: (606) 848-1646
www.uky.edu/~rsilver/
CommunityService/ky-coal.htm

Open: Year round; closed some holidays. 10:00 A.M.–5:00 P.M. Monday–Saturday, 1:00–4:00 P.M. Sunday.

Info: Benham was originally a company town owned by International Harvester; the museum is located in the former company commissary. Photographs, memorabilia, videos, and scale models are used to present the story of coal mining in Kentucky. See the floor plan of a typical underground coal mine, and view displays on the formation of coal. (A personal collection of country music legend Loretta Lynn is displayed on the third floor of the museum.) A walking

mine tour is available in Lynch, 2 miles away.

Admission: Adults $3.00, children and students $1.00, seniors $2.00.

Directions: The museum is located in Benham, which is on State Highway 160, just east from its intersection with U.S. 119.

LYNCH

Mine Tour

Portal 31 Walking Tour
Tri-City Chamber of Commerce
Cumberland, KY 40823
Phone: (606) 589-5812
www.uky.edu/~rsilver/
CommunityService/ky-coal.htm

Open: Year round; closed some holidays. 10:00 A.M.–5:00 P.M. Monday–Saturday, 1:00–4:00 P.M. Sunday.

Info: The mine tour is presented in association with the Kentucky Coal Mine Museum (see previous listing). Lynch, located 2 miles from Benham, was originally a company town owned by U.S. Steel. The walking tour takes you through the surface buildings and structures built in Lynch to serve Mines 30, 31, and 32. An underground tour will be added in the near future.

Admission: See previous listing.

Directions: The mine is located in Lynch, KY, 2 miles east of Benham, KY. Benham is on State Highway 160, just east from its intersection with U.S. 119.

SECTION 3: Special Events and Tourist Information

TOURIST INFORMATION

State Tourist Agency

Kentucky Department of Travel
Capital Plaza Tower
500 Mero St., #22
Frankfort, KY 40601-5695
Phone: (800) 225-TRIP or
(800) 225-8747
E-mail: bbroks@exch.tour.state.ky.us
www.kentuckytourism.com

LOUISIANA

State Gemstone: Agate

No information available.

SECTION 2: Museums and Mine Tours

NEW ORLEANS

Museum 🏛

Louisiana Nature Center
P.O. Box 5
5601 Reed Blvd. (Joe Brown Park)
New Orleans, LA 70187
Phone: (504) 246-5672

Open: All year, closed holidays. Tuesday–Friday 9:00 A.M.–5:00 P.M., Saturday 10:00 A.M.–5:00 P.M., Sunday 12:00–5:00 P.M.
Info: The Nature Center has a small collection of gems and minerals on display.
Admission: Adults $4.75, seniors $3.75, children $2.50.
Directions: The museum is located in Joe Brown Park in the city of New Orleans.

SHREVEPORT

Museum 🏛

Louisiana State Exhibit Museum
P.O. Box 38356
3015 Greenwood Road
Shreveport, LA 71133
Phone: (318) 632-2020

Open: All year, closed holidays. Monday–Friday 9:00 A.M.–4:00 P.M., Saturday–Sunday 12:00–4:00 P.M.
Info: The museum has exhibits on mining and on salt domes.
Admission: Adults $2.00, children 6–17 $1.00, 5 and under free.
Directions: Take Interstate 20 to exit 6A; go north $1/10$ mile to Greenwood Road. Turn west onto Greenwood.

SECTION 3: Special Events and Tourist Information

TOURIST INFORMATION

State Tourist Agency

Louisiana Travel Promotion Association
P.O. Box 3988
Baton Rouge, LA 70821-3988
Phone: (800) 99GUMBO or
(800) 994-8626
www.state.la.us
www.louisianatravel.com

MISSISSIPPI

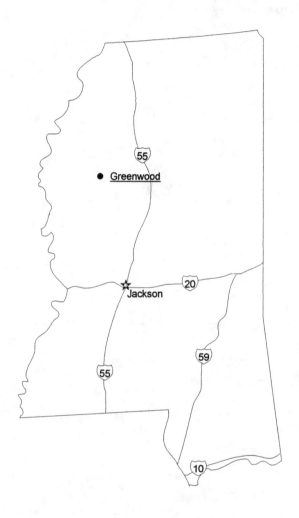

State Stone/Rock: Petrified Wood

SECTION 1: Fee Dig Sites and Guide Services

No information available.

SECTION 2: Museums and Mine Tours

GREENWOOD

Museum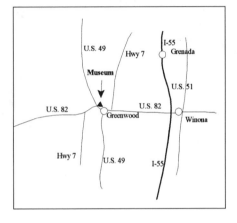

Cottonlandia Museum
1608 Highway 82 West
Greenwood, MS, 38930
Phone: (662) 453-0925; (800) 748-9064
(Greenwood Convention & Visitors
Bureau)

Open: Daily, closed major holidays.
Monday–Friday 9:00 A.M.–5:00 P.M.,
Saturday 2:00–5:00 P.M.
Info: The museum houses an exhibit of
rocks and minerals from Mississippi.
Admission: Adults $4.00, children 4–18

$1.00, college students $2.00, 65 and
older $3.50.
Directions: Located on U.S. 82 just west
of Park Avenue.

SECTION 3: Special Events and Tourist Information

TOURIST INFORMATION

State Tourist Agency

Mississippi Division of Tourist
Development
P.O. Box 22825
Jackson, MS 39205
Phone: (601) 359-3297 or
(800) 927-6378
www.mississippi.org

MISSOURI

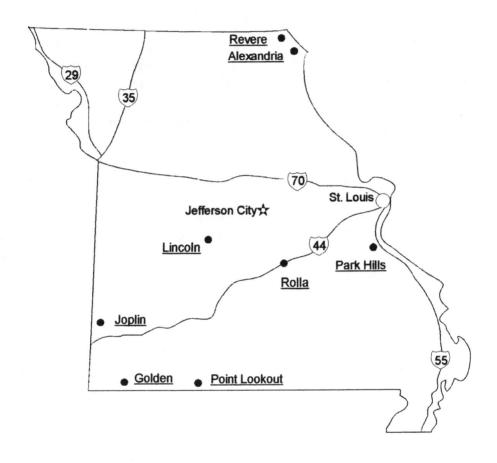

State Gemstone: Galena (1967)
State Stone/Rock: Mozarkite (1967)

SECTION 1: Fee Dig Sites and Guide Services

ALEXANDRIA / *Native • Easy to Moderate*

Geode Mine Digging 𝑇

The following gems or minerals may be found:

▪ **Crystal-lined geodes**

Sheffler Rock Shop
Betty Sheffler
R.R.1, Box 172
Alexandria, MO 63430
Phone: (660) 754-6443

Open: April 1–December 1 9:00 A.M.–5:00 P.M., 7 days/week (weather permitting). Call ahead for conditions at the mine, since weather affects digging at the mine.

Info: Geode mine digging; easily accessible strip mine. You can find geodes lined with minerals such as calcites, pyrites, barites, selenite needles, dolomite, sphalerite, kaoline, aragonite, goethite, and hematite. You must provide your own equipment; you will need a pry bar, pick, or rock hammer. A shovel may be useful.

Admission: $10.00 per person for 50 pounds of geodes; $0.50/pound for over 50 pounds. Clubs of 10 or more should make reservations 5 days in advance.

Other services available: Picnic area, free primitive camping, rock shop which includes display of opened geodes, mineral specimens, jewelry mountings, and rockhunting supplies.

Directions: On U.S. 61, 6 miles south of Alexandria.

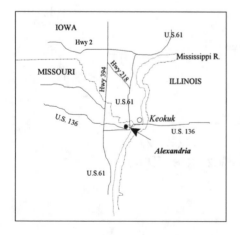

REVERE / *Native • Easy to Moderate*

Dig for Geodes 𝑇

The following gems or minerals may be found:

▪ **Geodes**

Geode Hollow Rock Shop and Mine
Wilbur and Norma Himes
R.R. 2, Box 23A
Revere, MO 63465
Phone: (660) 754-6347

Open: By appointment only.

Info: These geodes have smoky quartz and clear crystals with different miner-

Geodes

Geodes are round stones that have a crystal-filled hollow in the middle. They began as gas-filled bubbles in lava, or as soft areas in rock, which were eroded. Over time, water containing minerals seeped into the hollow and evaporated, leaving the minerals behind as crystals.

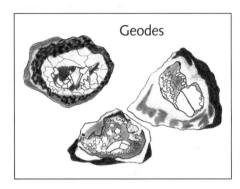

Geodes

The geodes from eastern Missouri are lined with a layer of chalcedony, a form of quartz, which holds the geode together. These geodes have clear and smoky quartz crystals inside, with different mineral buildups in them. The buildups could be clear or white calcite, iron pyrite, goethite, or pink dogtooth calcite with brown calcite crystals; some have fluorescent crystals.

als and calcite buildups in them. The buildups could be pink fans, white barrel calcite, iron pyrite, dew-drop diamonds, gothite, pink dogtooth calcite with brown calcite crystals; some have fluoresdite crystals. Bring your own equipment and protective clothing.

Admission: $20.00 per person for up to 50 pounds; $0.20/pound above 50 pounds. Children 8–12 dig for half rate; under 8 dig free.

Other services available: Rock shop sells retail and wholesale geodes whole or cut.

Directions: Located in St. Francisville, MO. From Donnellson, IA, take U.S. 218 to IA Route 394. Take 394 south across the toll bridge to St. Francisville. Look for signs. From Keokuk, IA, take U.S. 136 west to Wayland, MO. An unnumbered road goes north from Wayland to St. Francisville.

GOLDEN

Museum 🏛

Golden Pioneer Museum
Highway 86 and "J"
P.O. Box 216
Golden, MO 65658
Phone: (417) 271-3300

Open: Tuesday–Saturday 10:00 A.M.–5:30 P.M.

Info: The museum displays minerals from around the world, including what is reported to be the world's largest turquoise carving, made from a 68-pound stone. The museum also contains what is reported to be the largest double terminated single quartz crystal (1,250 pounds), a single cluster of quartz crystals weighing over 4,000 pounds, a large display of amethyst, fluorite crystals, and selenite clusters.

Admission: $2.00.

Directions: Located at the intersection of Highway 86 and "J," on Table Rock Lake, between Branson, MO, and Eureka Springs, AR.

JOPLIN

Museum 🏛

Everett J. Ritchie Tri-State Mineral Museum
Schifferdecker Park
P.O. Box 555
Joplin, MO 64802
Phone: (417) 623-2341
Fax: (417) 623-6393

Open: Tuesday–Sunday 9:00 A.M.–4:00 P.M., Sunday 1:00–4:00 P.M.

Info: The museum has exhibits of ore specimens and mining artifacts depicting the story of lead and zinc mining in the Tri-State (Kansas, Missouri, and Oklahoma) area.

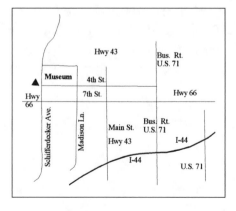

Admission: Free; donations accepted.

Directions: Located in the Joplin Museum Complex. From I-44, take exit 6 (Main Street, also State Highway 43), and turn north. Travel north to State Highway 66, then turn left (west). Travel to Schifferdecker Avenue, and turn right. The museum is one block north, on the left.

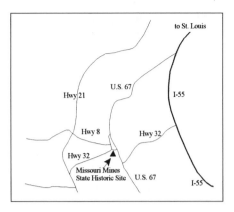

PARK HILLS

Museum 🏛

Missouri Mines State Historic Site
Highway 32, P.O. Box 492
Park Hills, MO 63601-0176
Phone: (573) 431-6226

Open: All year. 10:00 A.M.–4:00 P.M. Monday–Saturday. Noon–5:00 P.M. Sundays in winter; noon–6:00 P.M. Sundays in summer.

Info: The museum has 1,100 specimens of minerals, ores, and rocks on display. The collection is based on an original collection by Missouri's first great mineral collector, Fayette P. Graves. The mineral gallery has 27 cases, some of which are antique display cases built in 1920. Six of the cases contain a collection demonstrating the systematic classification of minerals. The museum also has a fluorescent mineral room, domi-nated by minerals from Franklin, NJ, zinc mines. There is also a display featuring Missouri minerals as well as specimens of other minerals easily collected in the state.

The museum has a gallery featuring some of the underground mining machinery used in area mines. In addition, some of the mining buildings at the museum complex are being restored, and historical interpretations and walking tour trails are being installed. The admission fee includes a tour of the site.

The area is known as the "Old Lead Belt." Lead mining occurred between 1864 and 1972, and the area was the nation's leading producer of lead for 60 of those years.

Admission: Adults $2.00, children (6–12) $1.25, children under 6 free.

Directions: On the south side of Highway 32, 1½ miles west of the junction with U.S. 67 in Park Hills.

POINT LOOKOUT

Museum 🏛

Ralph Foster Museum
College of the Ozarks
Point Lookout, MO 65726
Phone: (417) 334-6411

Open: 9:00 A.M.–4:30 P.M. Monday–Saturday when school is in session.
Info: The museum has several displays of minerals and rocks. These include a display of minerals in the Ozarks, which has varied types of quartz, jasper, graphite, mica, pyrite, copper, and others. There are also displays of many types of geodes, quartz crystals, and over 150 different minerals. There is a display of mineral spheres and of fluorescent minerals.
Admission: Adults $4.50, seniors $3.50, children free.
Directions: On the college campus in Point Lookout.

ROLLA

Museum 🏛

Mineral Museum—University of Missouri-Rolla
Department of Geology and Geophysics
125 McNutt Hall
Rolla, MO 65409-0410
Phone: (573) 341-4616
Fax: 341-6935

Open: Monday–Friday 8:00 A.M.–5:00 P.M. when school is in session.
Info: The museum has about 3,500 specimens of minerals, ores, and rocks from 92 countries and 47 states on display. The collection is based on an original collection from the state of Missouri exhibit displayed at the 1904 Louisiana Purchase Exposition, along with minerals donated by Mexico and the Missouri geology collection from the 1893 Chicago World Fair. Displays of gemstones and gold specimens from Peru are among the museum highlights.
Admission: Free.
Directions: On the university campus in Rolla.

SECTION 3: Special Events and Tourist Information

TOURIST INFORMATION

State Tourist Agency

Missouri Division of Tourism
Truman State Office Building
P.O. Box 1055
Jefferson City, MO 65102
Phone: (573) 751-4133; (800) 877-1234
www.missouritourism.org

NORTH CAROLINA

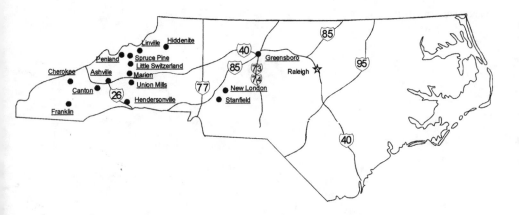

State Gemstone: Emerald (1973)

Introduction to Gem Mining in North Carolina: Cowee Valley Mines

The list of gems and minerals native to this valley in Franklin is said to include the following:

Rubies	Quartz crystal
Sapphires	Rutile
Rhodolite, almandite,	Kyanite
and pyrope garnet	Mica
Periodot	Feldspar
Almandite	Sillimanite
Moonstone	

Although Native Americans probably collected gemstones in the Cowee Creek Valley long before 1800, gemstones found in the valley in the gravel of the Caler Fork of Cowee Creek, a tributary of the Tennessee River, soon after the Civil War resulted in a systematic search of the area. Rubies and sapphires were found in the gravels of the Caler Fork for a distance of 3 miles. These finds led to commercial exploration by two developers in particular, the American Mining and Prospecting Co. and the United States Ruby Mining Co. These developers searched for the source of the gems found in the creek gravels; however, to this day, this source has never been discovered. One theory is that the gem-bearing matrix has completely washed out of the ancient Appalachian Mountains, and consequently there is no mother lode in the range. All that remains are the crystals that settled into the relatively protected beds of the valley.

There are only two places in the world where sandy gravel yields blood-red rubies. One is in the Mogok Valley in Burma, India, and the other is in the Cowee Valley of North Carolina. The blood-red rubies are considered to be more valuable than diamonds of equal quality.

The commercial ventures, meeting failure, pulled out of the area in the early 1900s, and the land was divided into small farms. The sands of the valley were never subjected to intensive commercial mining, thus leaving a wealth of material for the collector. In response, several mines opened to offer mining of gems from the Cowee Valley gravels.

Actually, calling them *mines* is somewhat misleading. There are no tunnels or shafts or any of the equipment associated with underground mining. The gem-bearing ore is located along the Caler Fork of Cowee Creek in a layer of mud, clay, and gravel, which varies from 2 to 10 feet in depth.

Most mine owners excavate the

ore in a shallow surface mine and supply the excavated ore to collectors in buckets or bags; the collector washes the same dirt he or she would have dug, but without the work of digging and transporting the ore to the flume. At the time of this writing, the authors have located only one mine in the Franklin area where a collector can still dig his or her own gem ore from the source. Including this mine, there are currently four mines where prospectors can screen natural gravel which the mine owners/operators say has not been salted or enriched.

SECTION 1: Fee Dig Sites and Guide Services

ALMOND / *Enriched Ore* • *Easy*

Pan for Gems *T*

The following gems or minerals may be found:

• Rubies, sapphires, amethyst, topaz, garnet, citrine, smoky quartz

Nantahala Gorge Ruby Mine
P.O. Box 159
U.S. 19 / U.S. 74
Almond, NC 28702
Phone: (828) 488-3854
Fax: (828) 488-3854

Open: Mid-May through mid-October, 10:00 A.M.–6:00 P.M., 7 days/week.
Info: Enriched native ore is sold by the bag.
Admission: Free. Ruby bags: 1 bag $3.00, 2 bags $5.00; sapphire bags: 1 bag $4.00, 2 bags $7.00; other bags from $20.00–$60.00.
Other services available: Gem cutting and mounting.

Directions: On U.S. 19/U.S. 74 between Bryson City and Andrews.

CANTON / *Native material* • *Easy*

Sluice for Gems *T*

The following gems or minerals may be found:

• Sapphires (pink, blue, gray, white, bronze)

Old Pressley Sapphire Mine
J.R.B. Mines, Inc.
240 Pressley Mines
Canton, NC 28716
Phone: (704) 648-6320

Open: April 1–October 31 (flume), all year (prospecting), 9:00 A.M.–6:00 P.M. 7 days/week.
Info: Buy buckets of ore from the mine (native stones only).
Admission: $5.00, 10-quart bucket of ore $0.50 each.

The Old Pressley Sapphire Mine is the source of the Star of the Carolinas, a 1,445-carat sapphire and the Southern Star, a 1,035 carat sapphire.

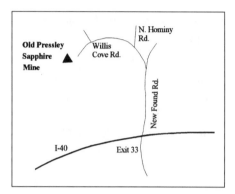

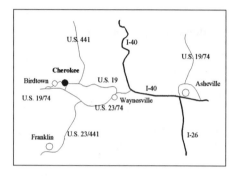

Prospecting April–October $10.00, November–March $7.00.

Other services available: Refreshments, restrooms, picnic area, mountain scenery, rock shop, souvenirs, RV and camping sites.

Directions: From I-40, take exit 33 and travel north on New Found Road. Follow signs to the mine.

CHEROKEE / *Enriched Native Ore* • *Easy*

Pan for Gold or Gems *T*

The following gems or minerals may be found:

- Rubies, sapphire, emerald, amethyst, topaz, garnet, citrine, smoky quartz, gold

Smoky Mountain Gold and Ruby Mine
Highway 441 North
Cherokee, NC 28719
Phone: (828) 497-6574

Open: All year. Hours: 9:00 A.M.–5:00 P.M. 7 days/week.

Info: Enriched native ore is sold by the bag or the bucket.

Admission: Free, 2 bags $7.00, buckets $5.00, 1 gallon $10.00, 5 gallon $50.00.

Other services available: Gems and rock shop.

Directions: Highway 441 North, in downtown Cherokee.

Mines in the Franklin Area:

FRANKLIN / *Native Material* • *Easy*

Sluice for Gems *T*

The following gems or minerals may be found:

• Rubies, sapphires, garnets (both rhodolite and pyrope), moonstones, rutile, sillimanite

Cherokee Mine
Clyde and Effie McCrackine
2586 Ruby Mine Road
Franklin, NC 28734
Phone: (828) 524-5684

Open: 8:00 A.M.–5:00 P.M., 7 days/week.

Info: Native gem-bearing soil dug from the mine is provided in buckets. Help is provided while you are sluicing.

Admission: Adults $6.00/day, children (6–11) $4.00/day, children under 6 free, 2-gallon bucket of soil $0.75 each.

Other services available: Restrooms, snacks.

Directions: Approximately 12 miles from Franklin. Take Highway 28 north from Franklin to Cowee Baptist Church. Just past the church, turn right on Cowee Valley Road. Stay on Cowee Valley Road to the fork of Ruby Mine Road

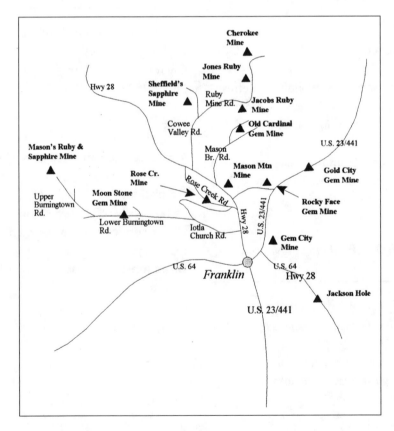

and Leatherman Gap Road. Turn right and follow Ruby Mine Road to the Cherokee Mine.

FRANKLIN / *Enriched Ore • Easy*

Sluice for Gems *T*

The following gems or minerals may be found:

• Rubies, sapphires, garnets, tourmaline, smoky quartz, amethyst, citrine, moonstone and topaz

Cowee Valley Ruby Mine
6771 Sylva Road (41 North)
Franklin, NC 28734
Phone: (828) 369-5271
Fax: (828) 524-0633

Open: 9:00 A.M.–5:00 or 6:00 P.M. 7 days/week.
Info: Soil containing gems native to the region and enriched material from elsewhere can be purchased and sluiced. Help is provided to beginners, and there is a covered, lighted flume for sluicing.
Admission: Free. Bags of ore, 6 for $5.00.
Other services available: Gem cutting, rock and mineral shop, clean restrooms.
Directions: North of Franklin on Highway 441.

FRANKLIN / *Native or Enriched Ore • Easy*

Sluice for Gems *T*

The following gems or minerals may be found:

• Rubies, sapphires, garnets, tourmaline, smoky quartz, amethyst, citrine, moonstone, topaz

Gem City Mine
c/o Ruby City Gems
44 East Main Street
Franklin, NC 28734
Phone: (828) 524-3967

Open: May 15–October 15, 9:00 A.M.–5:00 P.M., 6 days/week; 7 days/week in July and August.
Info: Soil containing gems native to the region and enriched material from elsewhere can be purchased and sluiced. Help is provided, and there is a covered flume for sluicing. The mine is associated with the Ruby City Gem Shop and Museum in Franklin.
Admission: $3.00, and get 1 free bag. Bags of ore $2.00, 3 bags $5.00.
Other services available: Clean restrooms.
Directions: One mile north of Franklin on Highway 441.

Mining in North Carolina

Essential equipment is provided by the mine: the flume, a trough with running water, and the sluice box, a wooden tray with a wire mesh screen for a bottom.

Mining at North Carolina mines basically involves putting a small amount of the gem ore (soil) in the sluice box, and then holding and gently shaking the box in the flume so that the dirt is washed away and the stones are left. The stones are then examined, and gems or minerals or stones that the miner wants are removed and placed in a container or small bag. The remaining material is dumped out, and more ore placed in the box and sluiced.

When mining in the natural soil, you may not always find a large quantity of stones, and those found may not be of gem quality or worth cutting. But for the true rockhound, the thrill is in knowing there is always the *possibility* that one may find that special gem or mineral at a mine, and searching until it is found. Many mines in the area have begun "enriching" or "salting" their native soil to provide additional material to find. Gems and minerals of pretty colors from around the world are mixed in with the ore in the bucket or bag. Children especially enjoy finding and identifying these added materials. When looking for a mine, ask if the gem-bearing soil is native or enriched. (See page 23 for a definition of *enriched* or *salted* material.)

FRANKLIN / *Enriched Native Ore* • *Easy*

Sluice for Gems *T*

The following gems or minerals may be found:

- Rubies, sapphires, garnets, emeralds, tourmaline, smoky quartz, amethyst, citrine, moonstone, topaz

Gold City Gem Mine
Curtis and Susan Rhoades

9410 Sylva Road, Highway 441 North
Franklin, NC 28734
Phone: (828) 369-3905; (800) 713-7767
Fax: (828) 524-0426
E-mail: goldcity@drake.dnet.net
www.goldcityamusement.com

Open: April–November, 9:00 A.M.–5:30 P.M., 7 days/week. Open Friday–Monday in March.

Info: Soil containing gems native to the region and enriched material from elsewhere can be purchased and sluiced. Help is provided, and there is a covered flume for sluicing, which has been specially constructed for handicapped needs.

Admission: Free, 5 buckets of basic dirt $5.00. Group and student rates are available.

Other services available: Clean restrooms, snacks and cold drinks, picnic tables, playground.

The jewelry and gift shop offers gifts and souvenirs, custom jewelry made on the premises, and jewelry repair. The country general store offers antiques, crafts, and collectibles. The chair lift and mountain top garden and waterfall offer a four-state view from the observation deck on the top of Cowee Mountain.

Directions: Six miles north of Franklin on Highway 441.

FRANKLIN / *Native or Enriched Ore* ▪ *Easy*

Sluice for Gems T

The following gems or minerals may be found:

▪ **Rubies, sapphires, garnets, tourmaline, smoky quartz, amethyst, citrine, moonstone, topaz**

Jackson Hole
Highway 28 North
Franklin, NC 28734
Phone: (828) 524-5850

Open: Summer 9:00 A.M.–6:00 P.M., 7 days/week. Winter 10:00 A.M.–4:00 P.M., Friday–Monday. Closed occasionally on Tuesday.

Info: Purchase soil containing gems native to the region and buckets of enriched material from elsewhere, and sluice for gems. Help is provided, and there is a covered flume for sluicing.

Admission: Free. Buckets of ore: Small: $6.00 each, 2 for $10.00. Ultimate: $30.00 each, 2 for $50.00. $100.00 bucket club gets $45.00 stone cut free and 10% off membership card.

Other services available: Clean restrooms, snack bar, gem shop, gem cutting.

Directions: East of Franklin on US 64 and Highway 28, halfway between Franklin and Highlands.

FRANKLIN / *Native only* ▪ *Easy*

Sluice for Gems T

The following gems or minerals may be found:

▪ **Rubies, sapphire, rhodolite garnets, rutile, sillimanite, and other precious stones**

Jacobs Ruby Mine
269 Deforest Lane *(mailing address)*
1305 Ruby Mine Road *(mine location)*
Franklin, NC 28734
Phone: (828) 524-7022
www.gemmines.com

Open: May 1–October 31, 9:00 A.M.–5:00 P.M. 6 days/week, closed Sunday.

In 1996, a woman found a 1½ pound sapphire in a 5-gallon bucket at the Mason Mountain Rhodolite and Ruby Mine.

Info: Sluice buckets of native gemstone gravel. All equipment furnished at no charge, and help is provided.

Admission: Adults $6.00, children (6–12) $3.00. Each admission fee receives two free buckets of gem-bearing gravel, extra buckets of gem dirt $0.50 each. Concentrate $19.75/5-gallon bucket.

Other services available: Umbrellas at no extra charge on a first-come, first-served basis, snacks and drinks, restrooms and changing rooms, free parking.

Directions: Take Highway 28 north from Franklin and turn right on Cowee Creek Road. Cowee Creek Road becomes Ruby Mine Road. Follow signs to the Jacobs Mine.

FRANKLIN / *Enriched and Native Ore* ▪ *Easy*

Sluice Buckets and Bags of Enriched Gem Dirt *T*

The following gems or minerals may be found:

▪ Rhodolite garnets, rubies, sapphires, kyanite, crystal quartz, smoky quartz, moonstones

Mason Mountain Rhodolite and Ruby Mine and Cowee Gift Shop

Brown and Martha Johnson
5315 Bryson City Road
Franklin, NC 28734
Phone: (828) 524-4570

Open: April 15–November 1, 8:00 A.M.–5:00 P.M., 7 days/week.

Admission: Adults $5.00/day, children under 12 $3.00/day. Buckets of gem dirt $1.00–$2.00 each, special bags of gem dirt $10.00 each, super buckets $50.00–$300.00 each.

Other services available: Gift shop, gem cutting (cabbing and faceting), crafts and jewelry, restrooms.

Directions: From Franklin take Highway 28 north approximately 5½ miles and look for the mine.

FRANKLIN / *Native Only* ▪ *Easy to Moderate*

Dig and Sluice for Gems *T*

The following gems or minerals may be found:

▪ **Sapphires (all colors) and pink and red rubies**

Mason's Ruby and Sapphire Mine
Christine Mason and Pete Civitello
583 Upper Burningtown Road
Franklin, NC 28734
Phone: (828) 369-9742

Open: April 1–October 31, 8:00 A.M.–5:00 P.M., 7 days/week.

Info: Only mine in the area where you can dig and sluice your own gem-bearing dirt. All equipment is furnished at no charge, and help is provided for beginners.

Admission: $10.00. Discounts only to clubs with 10 or more members.

Other services available: Picnic tables, modern bathroom facilities, free parking.

Directions: Take Highway 28 north from Franklin to Airport Road. Turn left, and follow signs to the mine.

FRANKLIN / *Native and Enriched Ore • Easy*

Sluice for Gems 𝑇

The following gems or minerals may be found:

• Rubies, sapphire, rhodolite, garnets, other precious stones

Moon Stone Gem Mine
Mr. Willard O. Holbrook
308 Lower Burningtown Road
Franklin, NC 28734
Phone: (828) 524-7764

Open: April 1–October 31, daylight to dark, 7 days/week.

Info: Sluice buckets of enriched native gemstone ore. All equipment is furnished at no charge. Help is provided.

Admission: $5.00, children under 6 free. 2-gallon bucket of gem dirt $1.00.

Directions: Take NC 28 north to the Big D Store, turn left immediately after store on Iotla Church Road. Stay on blacktop road approximately 8 miles, following signs to the mine.

FRANKLIN / *Enriched • Easy*

Sluice for Gems 𝑇

The following gems or minerals may be found:

• Rare native rhodolite, rubies, sapphires, garnets, topaz, moonstones, and others

The Old Cardinal Gem Mine
Jim and Edna Vest
71 Rockhaven Drive
Franklin, NC 28734
Phone: (828) 369-7534

Open: Year round; call first in January and February. 8:00 A.M.–5:00 P.M., 7 days/week.

Info: Enriched dirt is sold by the bag and bucket to be sluiced. Help is provided for beginners. All equipment is furnished. The flume is partly shaded.

Admission: Adults $5.00, children 5–12 $3.00, bags of gem dirt $2.00 each. Group rates are available.

Other services available: Picnic tables, clean restrooms, snacks, cold drinks, gift shop.

Directions: From Franklin take Highway 28 north approximately 5½ miles (watch for sign) to Mason Branch Road.

> Large gems including a 1,200-carat ruby and a 3,000-carat sapphire were found at the Rocky Face Mine.

Take a right. Go a few hundred yards, and look for the entrance sign for the mine.

FRANKLIN / *Enriched Native Ore* ▪ *Easy*

Sluice for Gems 𝑇

The following gems or minerals may be found:

▪ **Rubies, sapphires, rhodolyte garnets, and many other varieties**

Rocky Face Gem Mine
30 Saundertown Road
Franklin, NC 28734
Phone: (828) 524-3148

Open: April–October 31, 8:00 A.M.–5:00 P.M., 6 days/week; closed Sunday.
Info: Sluice 2-gallon buckets of enriched gem dirt. Sluicing is done at a covered concrete flume beside a tree-shaded creek.
Admission: Free. Bags of gem dirt: $4.00. Buckets: $5.00–$100.00.
Directions: 3 miles north of Franklin on U.S. 441; 300 feet off the highway on Saunderstown Road.

FRANKLIN / *Native or Enriched as Indicated* ▪ *Easy to Moderate*

Dig and Sluice for Gems 𝑇

The following gems or minerals may be found:

▪ **Rubies, sapphires, garnets, moonstones, amethysts, smoky quartz, citrine, rose quartz, topaz**

Rose Creek Mine, Campground, Trout Pond, and Rock Shop
The Martinez Family
115 Terrace Ridge Road
Franklin, NC 28734
Phone: (828) 524-3225
Fax: (828) 349-3774
E-mail: cazador@smnet.net
www.shipwreckcoins.com/rose.htm

Open: April–October, 9:00 A.M.–5:00 P.M., 7 days/week.
Info: Mine for gems in predug dirt or dig your own in the gem tunnel.* Help is provided for beginners, and there is a covered flume for panning rain or shine.
Admission: Adults $5.00 (includes one free bucket), children $3.00 (includes one free bucket), bags of gem dirt $1.00 each, buckets $2.00, super buckets and concentrates $5.00–$25.00. Group rates are available.

* Gem tunnel: dirt from the mine is

placed in covered shed for digging.
Other services available: Free coffee, clean restrooms, snacks, picnic tables.

Rainbow Trout Pond: $3.00/pound live weight. Bait and tackle provided. No catch and release. Discounts when you mine. Group rates available.

Rose Creek Campground: Tent sites; swimming pool; clean hot showers; wooded campsites; firewood; dump station; pets welcome on leash; playground; horseshoes; basketball; phone.

Camping rates: $15.00 per night, $90.00 per week, $270.00 per month. Includes all hookups (water, electric, sewer, and TV). Extra adults $2.00 each per night.

Directions: Take Highway 28 north from Franklin. Turn left on Rose Creek Road at the Little Tennessee River.

FRANKLIN / *Native and Enriched as Indicated* • *Easy*

Sluice for Gems 𝑇

The following gems or minerals may be found:

• **Native rubies and sapphires, and enriched material from around the world**

Sheffield Mine
385 Sheffield Farm Road
Franklin, NC 28734
Phone: (828) 369-8383
E-mail: ruby@dnet.net
www.intertekweb.com/Sheffield/index.html

Open: April–October 31, 9:00 A.M.–5:00 P.M., 7 days/week.

Info: There are two mines: the Sheffield Flume Mine for native ore only, and the Rainbow Mine with only enriched ore. Help in identifying gems is provided for beginners. All equipment is furnished. Sluicing is done at a partly shaded 150-foot flume.

Admission: $7.00/day. *Sheffield Flume Mine:* 2-gallon buckets of gem-bearing clay directly from the mine $0.50. *Rainbow Mine* (separate flume for enriched materials from around the world): $3.00 per bucket of gem dirt. Group rates are available.

Other services available: Clean rest rooms, snacks and cold drinks, picnic tables.

Directions: Take Highway 28 north from Franklin to Cowee Valley Road. Take Cowee Valley Road to Leatherman Gap Road. Look for signs to mine.

HIDDENITE / *Native or Enriched* • *Easy to Moderate*

Dig and Sluice for Gems 𝑇

The following gems or minerals may be found:

• **Sapphires, garnets, emeralds, hiddenite, smoky quartz, rutile, tourmaline, clear quartz, aquamarine, sillimanite, and others**

Emerald Hollow Mine—Hiddenite Gems, Inc.

What is Hiddenite?

Hiddenite is a transparent, emerald-green variation of the mineral spodumene. Spodumene is a member of a group of rocks known as pyroxenes and occurs in granite pegmatites, together with minerals such as tourmaline and beryl. Hiddenite is found *only* in Alexander County and is rarer and more valuable than emerald.

Mike and Dottie Watkins
P.O. Box 276
Hiddenite, NC 28636
Phone: (828) 632-3394

Open: March–December each year, 8:30 A.M. to sunset or 7:30 P.M., 7 days/week; closed Christmas.

Info: Sluice for gems in buckets of pre-dug dirt, dig your own, or search for gems in the creek. Help is provided, and there is a covered flume for sluicing.

Admission: Combinations (digging, sluicing, creekin') $10.00/day, sluicing with one bucket of ore $5.00, "Creekin'"/sluicing with one bucket of ore $7.00/day. Buckets of native ore $3.00, other buckets of ore from $1.50 to $100.00. Group and special student rates are available.

Other services available: Snacks, picnic tables, lapidary shop, gift shop, restrooms.

The mine also offers special educational programs for students, guided by a former NC State geologist. The trip includes surface collection, searching creeks for gems, and sluicing a bucket of ore.

Directions: From Interstate 40, turn west on NC 90 toward Taylorville. Hiddenite is approximately 12 miles from I-40. In Hiddenite, turn right on Sulphur Springs Road (State Road 1001), and follow the green signs. Hiddenite Gems, Inc. is on the right.

LITTLE SWITZERLAND / *Enriched Native Ore* ▪ *Easy*

Sluice for Gems *T*

The following gems or minerals may be found:

▪ Sapphire, emeralds; rubies; aquamarine; tourmaline; topaz; garnets; amethyst; clear, rose, rutilated, and smoky quartz; lepidolite; citrine; beryl; moonstone, and kyanite

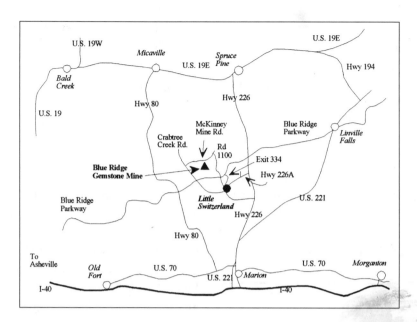

Blue Ridge Gemstone Mine &
Campground
Richard Johnson
P.O. Box 327, McKinney Mine Road
Little Switzerland, NC 28749
Phone: (828) 765-5264
Fax: (828) 765-2244
E-mail: dick-j@msn.com
www.dick-j.com

Open: April–December, 9:00 A.M.–5:00
P.M., 7 days/week.
Info: Sluice enriched gem-bearing soil.
All equipment is supplied, and help is
available. Sluice at a 330-foot flume,
which is enclosed and heated in spring
and fall.

Admission: Free. Buckets $5.00–100.00
("mother lode"). For a small fee
($30.00–35.00), staff will cut, grind, and
polish the stones you find and set them
into handcrafted settings.

Other services available: Museum, picnic area, handicapped access. Rock and
gift shop offering mining material, cut
gems, finished jewelry, 14k gold and sterling silver mounts, chains and bracelets,
lapidary equipment, services of a G.I.A.-
trained gemologist.

Campground: Features full hookups;

A "mother lode" bucket from the Blue Ridge Gemstone Mine yield-
ed a rough sapphire that cut into a 300+-carat star sapphire plus 11
smaller cut stones.

water and electricity; and primitive campsites.

Directions: Exit the Blue Ridge Parkway at Little Switzerland (exit 334). Take the first right (before the stop sign). Turn right onto Chestnut Grove Church Road, and go under the parkway, then drive for 1 mile. Turn left onto McKinney Mine Road. Blue Ridge Gemstone Mine is 2 miles down on the left.

LITTLE SWITZERLAND / *Enriched Native Ore • Easy*

Sluice for Gems T

The following gems or minerals may be found:

• **45 different rocks, minerals, and gems, including rubies, sapphires, aquamarine, emeralds, garnets, smoky quartz, beryl, uranium, and fluorescent minerals**

Emerald Village
P.O. Box 98
McKinney Mine Road
Little Switzerland, NC 28749-0098
Phone: (828) 765-6463
Fax: (828) 765-4367

Open: April 1–November 30, 9:00 A.M.– 5:00 P.M., 7 days/week. From Memorial Day to Labor Day, 9:00 A.M.–6:00 P.M.

Info: Emerald Village is located at two gem mines: Big McKinney and Bon Ami Mines. See Section 2 on Mine Tours for more information. Sluice enriched gem-bearing soil at a shaded flume. All equipment is supplied, and help is available.

Admission: Free. Buckets range in price from $6.00 to $500.00. Group rates available by reservation only.

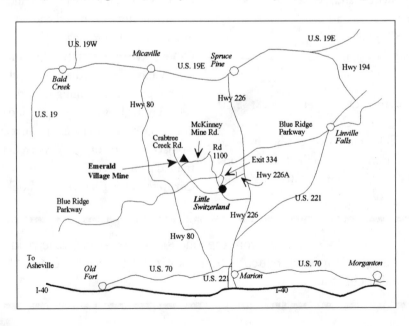

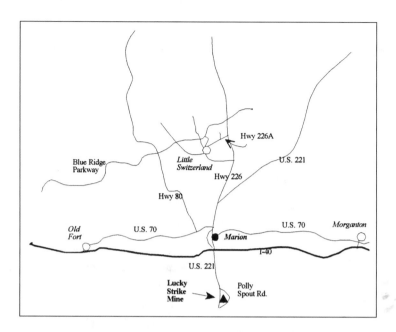

Other services available: North Carolina Mining Museum; mine tour; picnic area; snacks and drinks; restrooms; cab and facet shop; gemstone identification; gem cutters at work; rock and gift shop offering mining material, cut gems, finished jewelry, rocks and minerals, souvenirs, lapidary equipment.

Directions: Take exit 334 (Little Switzerland) off the Blue Ridge Parkway. At the bottom of the exit ramp, turn right onto Chestnut Grove Road and go under the parkway. Drive approximately 1 mile to the end of the road, then turn left onto McKinney Mine Road. The museum is at Emerald Village, 2 miles down the road, on the right.

MARION / *Enriched Ore • Easy*

Sluice for Gems or Pan for Gold *T*

The following gems or minerals may be found:

▪ **Gold and gemstones**

The Lucky Strike
Liz McCormick
Route 5, Box 733
Polly Spout Road
Marion, NC 28737
Phone: (828) 738-4893

Open: All year, Monday–Saturday 9:00 A.M.–6:00 P.M., Sunday 1:00–5:00 P.M.

Info: All equipment is supplied, and help is available. Instructions on panning is provided. Dredges and sluice boxes are available for rent.

Admission: Free. Small fee for buckets.
Other services available at the mine: Restaurant, campground.
Directions: 5.3 miles south of I-40 on Route 221, then turn left on Polly Spout Road.

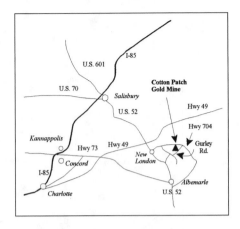

NEW LONDON / *Placer Material* ▪ *Easy to Moderate*

Pan for Gold *T*

The following gems or minerals may be found:

▪ Gold

Cotton Patch Gold Mine
Donald and Francene Reeves
41697 Gurley Road
New London, NC 28127
Phone: (704) 463-5797

Open: March–October each year, 9:00 A.M.–5:00 P.M., Tuesday–Sunday. Open holiday Mondays.
Info: Much of the work conducted at the Cotton Patch Mine involved recovery of gold from placer material. In 1958 a trench was opened on the property, and in 1961 the mine was opened to the public for panning and mineral collecting. In 1987 one of the shafts dug on a large quartz vein was reopened. This material is occasionally mixed with the placer material, and visitors usually have good results when panning.

Panning fee: $7.00 for 5 buckets of dirt (no sharing; no doggie bags). Fee entitles one to washed ore, panning equipment, and instruction. Group rates are available.
Other services available: General store, sandwiches and snacks, complete line of prospecting equipment, souvenirs, picnic area.
Campground: Rates: Wilderness/tent $10.00 per night for 2 people, hookups 16.00 per night for 2 people, air conditioning/heat 2.00 per night, extra person 2.00 each per night. Monthly rates available.
Directions: From New London, take State Highway 740 east toward Badin. Gurley Road will be on the right, shortly after leaving New London. Turn right on Gurley Road to get to the mine.

Gems from the Cowee Valley and Around the World

The Cowee Valley remains a location where natural precious gemstones can be found, but is also a location where you can learn identification of gem specimens from around the world.

The lure of gems has brought people to the Cowee Valley for over 400 years, beginning with Spanish explorers in the 1500s. In recent times, the area has seen the growth of the tourism industry and many "salted" mines have sprung up. These "salted" locations may be actual mine sites or just a flume line set up alongside the road. At these "mines" you can sluice for gemstones from around the world. Besides the educational value of identifying these finds, some of the material can be cabbed or faceted. In addition, they provide practice for sluicing native materials.

On a recent trip to the Cowee Valley, after only two hours of sluicing, the author's 11-year-old daughter found a 12-carat sapphire which could be cabbed to a 7½ carat gem. The authors also found several smaller facetable sapphires—proving to them, at least, that there are natural gems to be found at the mines. While mining, the authors saw another gentleman who had just found a beautiful pigeon-blood-red ruby.

SPRUCE PINE / *Enriched Native Ore • Easy*

Sluice for Gems 𝑇

The following gems or minerals may be found:

• Sapphire, crabtree emeralds, Wiseman and Brushy Creek aquamarine, rubies, tourmaline, topaz, garnets, amethyst, citrine, moonstone

Gem Mountain Gemstone Mine
Charles and Kay Buchanan
P.O. Box 488, Highway 226

Spruce Pine, NC 28777
Phone: (828) 765-6139; (888) 817-5829
E-mail: gemmtn@m-y.net
www.gemmountain.com

Open: All year except January and February. 9:00 A.M.–5:00 P.M. until Memorial Day, 9:00 A.M.–7:00 P.M. until Labor Day, 7 days/week. Closed Christmas Day.

Info: Sluice enriched gem-bearing soil provided in buckets. All equipment is furnished.

Admission: Free. 2-gallon bucket of ore:

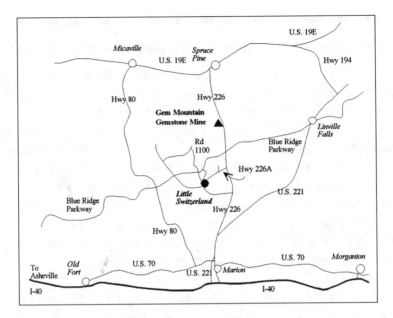

start at $7.00 each, other sizes and prices of buckets available up to $100.00. Two stones cut free with $100.00 bucket.

The mine also offers "dig your own" tours at 10:00 A.M. every Saturday from June 1 to August 31. This is a 3-hour trip to the Brushy Creek Aquamarine Mine. Look for stones such as golden beryl, tourmaline, garnet, and aquamarine, and keep what you find. Each trip is headed by a trained guide. Transportation, safety glasses, and pick hammer are furnished and are included in the trip fee.

Tour fee: Adults $50.00, children under 12 $25.00.

Other services available: Displays of local minerals and specimens from all over the US and the world, gem cutting, jewelry making, gift shop, sandwich and ice cream shop, picnic area.

Sands of Time Museum featuring maps and artifacts relating to the origins of human beings, their development and culture. Open 7 days/week from March through November. Groups welcome.

Directions: Located between Spruce Pine and the Blue Ridge Parkway, 1 mile north of the North Carolina Mineral Museum.

SPRUCE PINE / *Enriched Native Ore • Easy*

Sluice for Gems

The following gems or minerals may be found:

• Emeralds; rubies; aquamarine; tourmaline; topaz; garnets; amethyst; rose, clear, rutilated, and smoky quartz; citrine; and beryl

Spruce Pine Area Mines

Another major gem-hunting area in North Carolina is Spruce Pine in Mitchell County. Just as the Cowee Valley is known for rubies and sapphires, the Spruce Pine area is known for emeralds and aquamarine. The only working emerald mine in North America is in Mitchell County. Approximately 250 different kinds of minerals and gems are found there. About 46% of the feldspar used in the production of porcelain, china, and glass in the U.S. comes from Mitchell County. The following gems and minerals are said to be found in mines in the Spruce Pine area:

Beryl (including emerald)	Oligoclase
	Moonstone
Hyalite	Apatite
Autunite	Uranium minerals
Torbernite	Kyanite
Tourmaline	Quartz, rose and
Garnet	smoky
Columbite	Actinolite
Sphalerite	Spodumene
Thulite	Talc
Epidote	Aquamarine
Amethyst	Citrine
Hiddenite	

Rio Doce Gem Mine
Jerry and Geruza Call
P.O. Box 296
Little Switzerland, NC 28749
Phone: (828) 765-2099

Open: April 1–first week in November, 9:00 A.M.–5:00 P.M., 7 days/week.

Info: Sluice enriched gem-bearing soil. The gem material is from local area mines and from famous mines in Brazil. All equipment is supplied, and help is available.

Admission: Free. Buckets $10.00–$100.00 each; with $50.00 bucket one gem cut free; with $100.00 bucket two gems cut free.

Other services available at the mine: Picnic area, free stone identification, gem and gift shop, mineral specimens, gem cutting school, rough stones, gem cutting, jewelry.

Directions: On Highway 226, ½ mile north of the Blue Ridge Parkway.

SPRUCE PINE / *Enriched Native Ore • Easy*

Sluice for Gems *T*

The following gems or minerals may be found:

▪ 31 different gems, including emeralds, rubies, aquamarine, tourmaline, topaz, garnets, amethyst, smoky quartz, citrine, and beryl

Note: Numerous gem, mineral, and/or lapidary stores in each of the two NC mining areas (Franklin and Spruce Pine) have collections of native gemstones (both uncut and cut) and native minerals on display so you can view rough stones before mining. You can also bring your stones for evaluation, cutting, and mounting. Check with the Chamber of Commerce or look in the phone directory in the area of interest.

Spruce Pine Gem and Gold Mine
Spruce Pine Gem and Mineral Center
Intersection of Blue Ridge Parkway and Highway 226
Route 1, Box 811
Spruce Pine, NC 28777
Phone: (828) 765-7981

Open: All year, winter 10:00 A.M.–5:00 P.M., summer 9:00 A.M.–6:00 P.M., Days: Monday–Saturday.
Info: Use an indoor flume with heated water to sluice enriched gem-bearing soil provided in buckets. All equipment is furnished, and help is available.
Admission: Free. Buckets $10.00, $20.00, $40.00, $100.00, and $500.00.
Other services available: Gem cutting and setting.
Directions: Exit 331 off the Blue Ridge Parkway on Highway 226 (next to the Mineral Museum).

STANFIELD / *Mine Tour ▪ State Historic Site*

Pan for Gold T

The following gems or minerals may be found:

- **Gold**

Reed Gold Mine Historic Site
9621 Reed Mine Road
Stanfield, NC 28163
Phone: (704) 721-4653
Fax: (704) 721-4657
E-mail: reedmine@ctc.net

Open: April 1–October 31, Monday–Saturday 9:00 A.M.–5:00 P.M.., Sunday 10:00 A.M.–5:00 P.M. November 1–March 31, Monday–Saturday 10:00 A.M.–4:00 P.M., Sunday 1:00–4:00 P.M.
Info: Gold panning is available only during the summer months (April through October) and closes at 4:00 P.M. See full entry in Section 2 for details on the Reed Gold Mine Historic Site.
Panning fees: $2.00/pan of ore. Instruction included.
Directions: From Charlotte, take Interstate 85 north, take exit for Highway 49

North (also the exit for UNC-Charlotte). Follow the highway past the university. After traveling for approximately 20 miles, take the off-ramp on the right for Highway 601. At the top of the ramp, turn left on Highway 601 south for 5 miles, then turn left onto Highway 200. This turn is marked with a brown State Historic Site sign. Follow Highway 200 for about 4 miles, then turn right on Reed Mine Road (another brown sign). The site is 2 miles down the road.

An alternative route is to take Highway 51 north through Matthews and Mint Hill. Highway 51 ends at an intersection with Highways 24/27 (Albemarle Road). Turn right at this intersection and follow Highway 24/27 for approximately 15 miles. You will cross Highway 601 and continue beyond it for 2 miles. When you cross the bridge over Rocky River, Reed Mine Road will be on the left immediately after the bridge. Turn left onto Reed Mine Road, and the site will be on the right 3 miles down the road.

UNION MILLS / *Easy*

Pan for Gold and Gemstones *T*

The following gems or minerals may be found:

- Gold, gemstones

Thermal City Gold Mining Company
Lloyd Nanny, Owner
5240 U.S. 221 N. Highway
Union Mills, NC 28167

Phone: (828) 286-3016;
(828) 287-2545 (night)
Fax: (828) 286-4264
www.HuntForGold.com
E-mail: jnanney@blueridge.net

Open: 7 days/week, 8:00 A.M.–dark.
Info: Site of a family-operated 1830s-era gold mine. Fine gold and an occasional nugget are found; a 7.26-ounce nugget was found in 1993. The site consists of a ½-mile section of the Second Broad River and about 30 acres of placer gravel deposits. Panning material for gold panning is brought up from the river using a backhoe, and this panning material is not enriched or salted. Gemstone panning material is salted with native material.
Panning fee: $5.00/day per person for gold panning. Gem buckets: $5.00–$50.00.
Common dig: A backhoe-fed wash plant will be used to extract gold from placer gravel. All concentrates will be hand panned. You receive clean gold in a bottle and black sands separately. All gold recovered will be split among participants according to GPAA (Gold Prospectors Association of America) methods.
Common dig schedule: Memorial Day, July 4th, Labor Day. Cost: $100.00/ miner. Operation requires minimum of 12 miners. Can be done for private groups.
The Annual Miners Meet is held Memorial Day weekend, with panning,

a treasure hunt, vendors, equipment demonstration, and other activities.

Other services available: Complete line of prospecting equipment, campground, riverside camping, hot showers, some sites have electricity.

Rates: $7.00/night for primitive sites, $10.00/night for limited power sites.

Directions: Take U.S. 221 (exit 85) off I-40 at Marion, and go south toward Rutherfordton for approximately 8 miles. Look for the sign on the left (Polly Spout Road), and follow the signs to the mine.

SECTION 2: **Museums and Mine Tours**

ASHEVILLE

Museum

Colburn Gem and Mineral Museum
2 South Pack Square
Asheville, NC 28802
Phone: (828) 254-7162
Fax: (828) 251-5652

Open: Tuesday–Saturday, 10:00 A.M.–5:00 P.M. all year; Sunday 1:00–5:00 P.M. (June–October)

Info: The Colburn Gem and Mineral Museum serves as a repository for gifts of mineral specimens. The museum opened in 1960 as a bequest of mineral collector Bernham Standish Colburn. Until 1982 it was operated by the Southern Appalachian Mineral Society; it is now a nonprofit corporation.

Collections include mineral specimens from North Carolina and the world and include gemstones, rocks, fossils, micromounts, minerals, and related artifacts. On view are a 229-carat cut blue topaz and a 376-pound aquamarine crystal; mineral treasures from North Carolina include the rare gem hiddenite.

The museum contains a large collection of photographs and slides depicting minerals and the history of mining in North Carolina. The museum's library contains over 500 volumes, publications, and manuscripts.

The museum holds an annual rock and mineral sale every August.

Admission: Adults $4.00, children 4–15 $3.00.

Directions: From Interstate 240, take exit 5A/Merrimon Avenue, and follow the signs for Highway 25 South for three blocks to Pack Square. From Interstate 40, take exit 50 (Highway 25, South Asheville) and continue on Highway 25 north through Biltmore Village for three miles. Parking is available streetside or in the parking garage adjacent to Pack Square. Handicapped accessible.

FRANKLIN

Museum

Franklin Gem and Mineral Museum
2 W. Main Street
Franklin, NC 28734
Phone: (828) 369-7831

Open: May–October, 10:00 A.M.–4:00 P.M.

Info: The museum is located in the old Franklin jailhouse on the square. It is operated by the Gem and Mineral Society of Franklin, NC, Inc.

Collections include mineral specimens from North Carolina and the world and feature gemstones, rocks, micromounts, minerals, and related artifacts.

Admission: Free.

Directions: On West Main Street in Franklin. Parking is available streetside or in the parking lot.

FRANKLIN

Museum

Ruby City Gems
44 East Main Street
Franklin, NC 28734
Phone: (828) 524-3967

Open: May 15–October 15, 9:00 A.M.–5:00 P.M. 6 days/week.

Info: The museum is located in the Ruby City Gem Shop on East Main Street, and can be entered from the shop.

The museum features a collection of 500 spheres, cut, ground, and polished by the original owner of the Gem Shop. In addition, there is a collection of fluorescent minerals, local and state minerals, and fossils and Indian artifacts.

Admission: Free.

Directions: On East Main Street in Franklin.

GREENSBORO

Museum

Natural Science Center of Greensboro
4301 Lawndale Drive
Greensboro, NC 27455
Phone: (336) 288-3769
Fax: (336) 288-0545
E-mail: nscg@greensboro.com
www.greensboro.com/sciencecenter

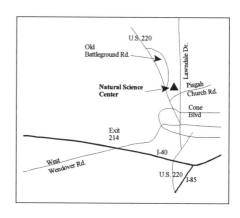

Open: All year, 9:00 A.M.–5:00 P.M.; Sunday 12:30–5:00 P.M., 7 days/week.
Info: The collection of minerals is located in the Geology Gallery. There are over 50 faceted NC mineral specimens on display.
Admission: Adults $5.00, children 4–13 $4.50, seniors $4.50.
Directions: Off U.S. 220, on the north side of the city.

HENDERSONVILLE

Museum 🏛

Mineral & Lapidary Museum of Henderson County, Inc.
400 N. Main Street
Hendersonville, NC 28792
Phone: (898) 698-1977

Open: All year, 1:00–5:00 P.M., 7 days/week.

Info: Exhibits cover mineralogy, geology, paleontology, and associated lapidary art.
Admission: Free.
Directions: Call for directions.

LINVILLE

Museum 🏛

Grandfather Mountain Nature Museum
P.O. Box 129
Linville, NC 28646
Phone: (828) 733-4337; (828) 733-2013; (800) 468-7325
E-mail: nature@grandfather.com
www.grandfather.com

Open: All year 8:00 A.M.–5:00 P.M., April–Labor Day 8:00 A.M.–7:00 P.M., 7 days/week. Closed Thanksgiving and Christmas.

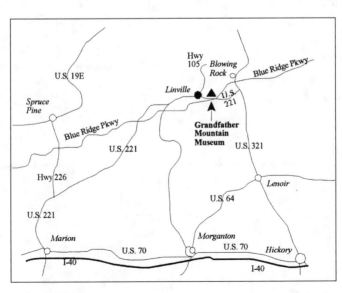

Info: Grandfather Mountain has been singled out by the United Nations as a biosphere reserve because of its significance to the biodiversity of the planet. It is a privately owned and protected wildlife sanctuary, which is home to 42 rare or endangered species.

The nature museum exhibits represent most of the historically important mines and miners of the last 100 years. Through these exhibits the history of rockhounding in NC is traced. Each specimen is identified as to where and by whom it was found.

Displays include most of the gems and minerals found in NC, organized by common mineral families and location. Families include quartz, garnet, radioactives, kyanite, beryl, and corundum; locations include the Foote Mineral Co. in Kings Mt. and the Hiddenite area. The exhibit includes choice NC specimens with a focus on emeralds and the largest amount of NC gold on display to the public in the state.

Admission: Adults $10.00, children 4–12 $5.00, children under 4 free. Group rates available.

Other services available: Nature shop, family restaurant, hiking and picnicking, highest suspension footbridge in America.

Directions: Off U.S. 221 one mile south of the Blue Ridge Parkway, and two miles north of Linville.

LITTLE SWITZERLAND

Museum/Mine Tour

North Carolina Mining Museum and Mine Tour
Emerald Village, Inc.
P.O. Box 98
Little Switzerland, NC 28749-0098
Phone: (828) 765-6463
Fax: (828) 765-4367

Open: April 1–Memorial Day, 9:00 A.M.–5:00 P.M.; Memorial Day–Labor Day 9:00 A.M.–6:00 P.M.; Labor Day–November 30 9:00 A.M.–5:00 P.M., 7 days/week.

Info: Take a walking tour of a now-closed feldspar mine. The mine was originally developed by the Bon Ami Company to mine feldspar as an ingredient for its polishing cleaner. Quartz and mica were also found in the mine, along with a complex uranium mineral known as samarskite, specimens of which can be seen in the mine ceiling. Because of the presence of uranium minerals in the mine, many of the rocks contain trace amounts of uranium, making them highly fluorescent when exposed to ultraviolet light.

The museum tells the story of the miners, the mining, the ores and minerals found in the mine, the equipment used, and the Bon Ami Mining Company. There are displays of antique equipment, with explanations of how they operated. The displays are in the visitors

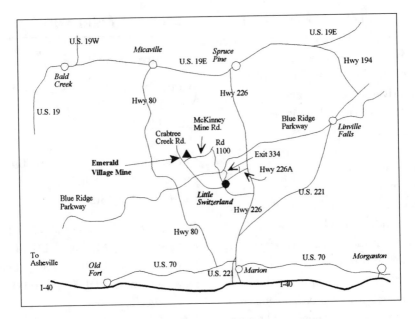

center, at the entrance to the mine, and inside part of the mine as well. Also included is a replica of a 1920s mining store.

Admission: Call for fees.

Directions: Take exit 334 (Little Switzerland) off the Blue Ridge Parkway. At the bottom of the exit ramp, turn right onto Chestnut Grove Road and go under the parkway. Drive approximately 1 mile to the end of the road, then turn left onto McKinney Mine Road. The museum is at Emerald Village, 2 miles down the road, on the right.

SPRUCE PINE

Museum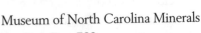

Museum of North Carolina Minerals
Route 1, Box 789
Milepost 331 on the Blue Ridge Parkway
Spruce Pine, NC 28777
Phone: (828) 765-2761

Open: All year, 9:00 A.M.–5:00 P.M. In summer, 7 days/week; in winter, closed Monday and Tuesday.

Info: The museum is operated by the National Park Service; specimens have been provided by local individuals and commercial enterprises.

The museum provides an introduction to the region's wealth of mineral resources. The primary focus is on min-

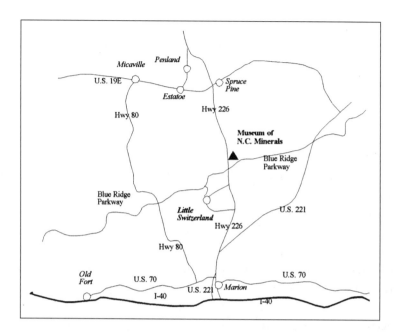

erals mined in the Spruce Pine district. Included are gemstones, fluorescent minerals, and rare radioactive rocks. Numerous semiprecious gemstones such as ruby, aquamarine, and emerald are shown in both rough and polished states. Featured are quartz, local gold, and several commercial rocks and minerals, including famed feldspar and tungsten. Various stages of refinement and everyday objects made from end products are displayed. The facing of the museum building itself is made of quartzite from a quarry on nearby Grandfather Mountain.

A visitors center operated by the Mitchell Chamber of Commerce located at the museum provides visitors with information about nearby attractions in western NC.

Admission: Free.

Directions: Located on State Highway 226 where it crosses under the Blue Ridge Parkway.

STANFIELD

Mine Tour/State Historic Site 🏛

Reed Gold Mine Historic Site
9621 Reed Mine Road
Stanfield, NC 28163
Phone: (704) 786-8331

Open: April 1–October 31, Monday–Saturday 9:00 A.M.–5:00 P.M., Sunday 11:00 A.M.–5:00 P.M. November 1–March 31, Monday–Saturday 10:00 A.M.–4:00 P.M., Sunday 1:00–4:00 P.M.

Info: Site of the first documented discovery of gold and the first intensive mining operation in the United States as part of the nation's first gold rush. The mine was in operation from 1803 to 1912. It was noted for the large size and purity of its gold nuggets. Gold discovery spread to nearby counties and into other southern states. North Carolina maintained a leadership in gold production until 1848, when it was eclipsed in importance by the great rush to California. Reed Gold Mine Historic Site is operated by the NC Department of Cultural Affairs, Division of Archives and History, Historic Section.

The site's visitors center features an introductory film and exhibits on historical events, gold mining processes, and equipment. Other features include:

Mine tour: A guided tour is conducted through a restored section of the old underground mine

Equipment tour: A tour is available of the 19th-century stamp mill used to crush ore (a mechanical engineering landmark).

Walking trails: Trails wind through the historic mining area past several shafts and tunnels and an exhibit interpreting the 1850s Engine House.

Admission: Free.

Directions: From Charlotte, take Interstate 85 north, take exit for Highway 49 north (also the exit for UNC-Charlotte). Follow the highway past the University. After traveling for approximately 20 miles, take the off-ramp on the right for Highway 601. At the top of the ramp, turn left on Highway 601 south for 5 miles, then turn left onto Highway 200. This turn is marked with a brown State Historic Site sign. Follow Highway 200 for about 4 miles, then turn right on Reed Mine Road (another brown sign). The site is 2 miles down the road.

SECTION 3: Special Events and Tourist Information

ANNUAL EVENTS

Macon County Gemboree, Franklin, NC 🐾

Held for 4 days in July

Admission: Adults $2.00, children under 12 free. Run-of-show ticket $5.00 (good for all days).

"Leaf-Looker" Gemboree, Franklin, NC 🐾

Held for 4 days in October

Admission: Adults $2.00, children under 12 free. Run-of-show ticket $4.00 (good for all days).

Info: Both events are sponsored by the Gem and Mineral Society of Franklin, NC, Inc., and by the Franklin Area Chamber of Commerce. Both are held at:

Macon County Community Building
U.S. 441 South
Franklin, NC

Both events offer rough and cut gems, minerals, jewelry, equipment, supplies, books, dealers, and exhibits.

For more information:
Franklin Area Chamber of Commerce
425 Porter Street
Franklin, NC 28734
Phone: (800) 336-7829; (828) 524-3161
www.franklin-chamber.com/mine1.html

Original North Carolina Mineral and Gem Festival, Spruce Pine, NC 🐾

Wholesale and retail shows held for 4 days at the end of July and the beginning of August. For information on the festival and on gem mines in Mitchell County, contact:

Mitchell County Chamber of Commerce
Route 1, Box 796
Spruce Pine, NC 28777
Phone: (704) 765-9483; (800) 227-3912
Fax: (704) 765-9483*51
E-mail: mitchamb@m-y/net
Info@mitchell-county.com
www.mitchell-county.com/north-carolina

TOURIST INFORMATION

State Tourist Agency 🐾

North Carolina Travel and Tourism Division
Department of Commerce
430 North Salisbury Street
Raleigh, NC 27603
Phone: (800) VISIT NC or (800) 847-4862

SOUTH CAROLINA

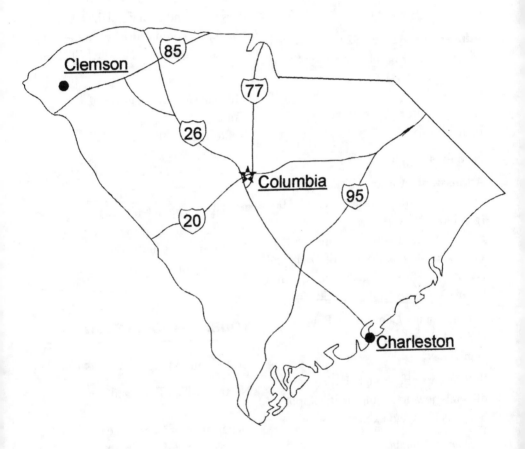

Clemson

85

77

26

Columbia

20

95

Charleston

Information not available.

CHARLESTON

Museum

Charleston Museum
360 Meeting Street
Charleston, SC 29403
Phone: (843) 722-2996

Open: All year, closed major holidays. Monday–Saturday 9:00 A.M.–5:00 P.M., Sunday, 1:00–5:00 P.M.

Info: The museum has a small display of gems and minerals, including some from Russia.

Admission: Adults $7.00, children (3–12) $4.00.

Directions: The museum is located in Charleston on Meeting Street at John Street.

CLEMSON

Museum

Bob Campbell Geology Museum
South Carolina Botanical Garden
Clemson University
Clemson, SC 29631
Phone: (864) 656-4600

Open: Thursday, Friday, Sunday 1:00 P.M.–5:00 P.M.; Saturday 10:00 A.M.–5:00 P.M. Call director for information.

Info: Displays include minerals, meteorites, and the largest faceted stone collection in the Southeast. Mineral specimens displayed are from both regional and worldwide locales. There is a reference collection of mineral species, and a library is available to researchers.

Admission: Call for rates.

Directions: The museum is located in the South Carolina Botanical Gardens, on the east side of the campus, off Perimeter Road.

COLUMBIA

Museum

McKissick Museum
University of South Carolina Campus
Columbia, SC 29208
Phone: (803) 777-7251

Open: All year, closed holidays. Monday–Friday 9:00 A.M.–4:00 P.M., Saturday–Sunday 1:00–5:00 P.M.

Info: The museum has exhibits on geology and gemstone exhibits.

Admission: Free.

Directions: The museum is located at the head of the Horseshoe area on the USC Campus, near Bull and Pendleton Streets.

COLUMBIA

Museum

South Carolina State Museum
301 Gervais Street
Columbia, SC 29201
Phone: (803) 737-4595

Open: All year, closed major holidays. Monday–Saturday 10:00 A.M.–5:00 P.M., Sunday 1:00–5:00 P.M.

Info: The museum has a displays of gems and minerals, mostly as part of other exhibits. Others are found as part of a hands-on natural history exhibit called NatureSpace.

Admission: Adults $4.00, children (6–17) $1.50, children under 6 free.

Directions: The museum is located in a former textile mill at the intersection of Gervais Street and Olympia Avenue. From I-26, take I-126 to Olympia Avenue. Turn south on Olympia. The museum will be on the right. From I-77, take exit 6, Shop Road, into Columbia. Shop Road will join Bluff Road (Hwy 48). Turn left on Olympia Avenue off Bluff Road, and drive to the museum.

SECTION 3: Special Events and Tourist Information

TOURIST INFORMATION

State Tourist Agency

South Carolina Division of Tourism
1205 Pendleton St. Box 71
Columbia, SC 29202
Phone: (803) 734-0235 or
(800) 346-3634
www.state.sc.us

TENNESSEE

State Gemstone: Tennessee River Pearls
State Stone/Rock: Limestone and Tennessee Marble

SECTION 1: Fee Dig Sites and Guide Services

No information available.

SECTION 2: Museums and Mine Tours

JOHNSON CITY

Museum 🏛

Hands On! Regional Museum
315 East Main Street
Johnson City, TN 37601
Phone: (423) 434-4263

Open: Tuesday–Friday 9:00 A.M.–5:00 P.M., Saturday 10:00 A.M.–5:00 P.M., Sunday 1:00–5:00 P.M. June–August only, Monday 9:00 A.M.–5:00 P.M.
Info: The museum is aimed at children. As part of its exhibits, it has a simulated coal mine.
Admission: Adults $5.00, children 3–18 $4.00, children under 2 free.

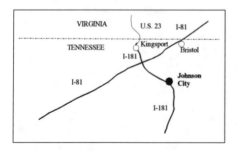

Directions: Take the Market Street exit off I-181 and drive west 1½ blocks to the museum.

MEMPHIS

Museum 🏛

Memphis Pink Palace Museum
c/o Memphis Museum System
3010 Central Avenue
Memphis, TN 38111-3399
Phone: (901) 320-6322
Fax: (901) 320-6391
www.memphismuseums.org

Open: Monday–Wednesday 9:00 A.M.– 4:00 P.M., Thursday 9:00 A.M.–8:00 P.M., Friday–Saturday 9:00 A.M.–9:00 P.M., Sunday 12:00–5:00 P.M.
Info: A geology exhibit with two parts: physical geology and historical geology. The physical geology exhibit covers meteorites, including the Allende meteorite, which predates our solar system; earthquakes; seismology; and mineral

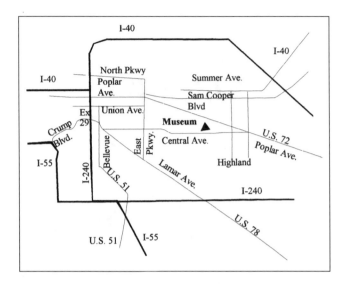

exhibits. The mineral exhibit includes minerals from around the world and cases of minerals from famous mid-South localities.

Admission: Adults $6.00, seniors $5.50, children 3–12 $4.50.

Directions: Take exit 29 off I-240 and drive east on Lamar Avenue. Take the left branch at the Y onto Central Avenue, and follow Central Avenue for several blocks. The museum will be on the left.

SECTION 3: Special Events and Tourist Information

TOURIST INFORMATION

State Tourist Agency 🖜

Tennessee Tourism
320 Sixth Avenue N.
Fifth Floor
Rachel Jackson Building
Nashville, TN 37243
Phone: (800) 836-6200; (888) 243-9769
www.state.tn.us

VIRGINIA

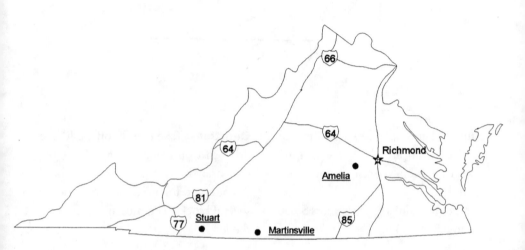

AMELIA / *Native ▪ Moderate to Difficult*

Dig for Beryls *T*
The following gems or minerals may be found:
▪ Beryl

Dick R. Boyles
13001 Butlers Road
Amelia, VA 23002-2905
Phone: (804) 561-2395

Open: All year; call for hours and days.
Info: Beryls range in color from clear to gray to gray-blue to green. Yellow and brown are also found. The mine is periodically excavated with a backhoe to uncover new material. You must provide your own equipment; you'll need a shovel, and a pick may be useful.
Admission: $3.00/person per day; pay at house (13001 Butlers Road—look for number on mailbox).
Directions: Call for directions. Amelia is located just off U.S. 360, southwest of Richmond.

AMELIA / *Native ▪ Easy to Difficult*

Dig for Gems and Minerals *T*
The following gems or minerals may be found:
▪ Beryl, agate, amazonite, calcite, fluorite, pyrite, quartz, rutile, topaz, tourmaline, mica, feldspar, phenakite, minerals in the tantalite/columbite series, and microcrystals

Morefield Gem Mine
13400 Butlers Road
Amelia, VA 23002
Phone: (804) 561-3399

Open: March–Christmas Eve. Summer: Tuesday–Saturday, spring/fall: Thursday–Saturday, 9:30 A.M.–4:30 P.M.
Info: Under new ownership since 1996, the mine is being expanded to improve its recreational aspects. Mine dump collecting, outcrop digging, and sluicing can all be done at the Morefield Mine.
Admission: Adults (13 and up) $8.00/person per day, children (12 and under) $6.00, children (3 and under) free. Group rates for groups of children with advance registration.
Other services available: Gift shop, gem cutting, vending machines, restrooms, picnic area.
Directions: Get on U.S. 360 west into Amelia County. 4.9 miles after crossing the Appomattox River, turn left onto County Road 628, and continue 1 mile south to the mine.

Fairy Stones

Fairy Stone State Park takes its name from the amazing little crystals called fairy stones. Formed and found within the park boundaries, these stone crosses are composed of iron aluminum silicate, which is called staurolite. Single crystals are hexagonal and often intersect at right angles to form Roman or Maltese crosses, or at other angles to form St. Andrew's crosses.

The formation of staurolite crystals involves an exact combination of heat and pressure such as that provided by the folding and crumpling of the earth's crust during the formation of the Appalachian Mountains. Certain types of rock that have been folded and crumpled in this manner are called schists. The staurolite crystals are usually harder than the surrounding schist and less easily weathered. As the staurolite-bearing schist is weathered away, the more resistant crystals are uncovered and come to lie on the surface. Occasionally staurolites can be found still embedded in their schist matrix.

The crystals are found in various schist bodies from New England southward through Virginia and into Alabama and Georgia. Staurolite is also reported to have been found in Montana. Colors range from light brown to dark brownish-black, and sometimes even a deep red. Staurolite has the habit of forming cross-like twinned crystals; 60° twins are most common; and exceptional 90° crosses are the most prized. Also found are staurolite rosettas, unusual specimens found when three crystals grow together to form a common center.

STUART / *Native • Easy to Moderate*

Hunt for Fairy Stones *T*

The following gems or minerals may be found:

• Staurolite crystals, also called fairy stones

Fairy Stone State Park
967 Fairystone Lake Drive

Stuart, VA 24171
Phone: (540) 930-2424
Fax: (540) 930-1136
www.state.va.us/-der/

Open: All year, daylight hours.
Info: No digging equipment is permitted. Bring a small container for your finds.
Admission: Free. Can take a small num-

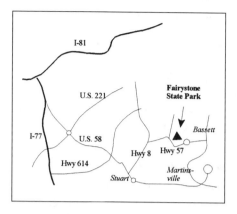

rentals; swimming Memorial Day to Labor Day (weather permitting).

State Park campground and cabins are available for use; to get more information or make a reservation, call (800) 933-7275.

Directions: Park is located off Highway 57 between Stuart and Bassett. To get to the fairy stone area, leave the park (Route 346) and turn left onto Route 57. Travel approximately 3 miles to the first service station (Haynes 57) on the left. The land on the left of the station is park property, and fairy stones may be hunted in that area.

ber of crystals for personal use; no commercial digging is permitted.

Other services available: Picnic area; hiking trails; restrooms; boat dock and

---

The Legend of Fairy Stones

It is said that long, long, ago fairies inhabited a certain quiet and remote region in the foothills of the Blue Ridge Mountains. The fairies roamed freely and enjoyed the beauty and serenity of that enchanted place.

One day they were playing in a sunny glade when an elfin messenger arrived from a city far, far away bearing the sad news of the death of Christ. When the fairies heard the terrible details of the crucifixion, they wept. As

Fairy Stones

their tears fell to the earth, they crystallized into little stone crosses. Though the fairies are no longer to be found there, the fairy stones remain in that enchanted spot as momentos of that day. *(Information courtesy of Fairy Stone State Park)*

SECTION 2: Museums and Mine Tours

MARTINSVILLE

Museum

Virginia Museum of Natural History
1001 Douglas Street
Martinsville, VA 24112
Phone: (540) 666-8600
E-mail: sfelker@vmnh.org
www.vmnh.org

Open: All year; closed major holidays.
Monday–Saturday 10:00 A.M.–5:00 P.M.,
Sunday 1:00–5:00 P.M.

Info: The museum has a large collection of rocks and minerals, and exhibits on mining. The Rock Hall of Fame presents the rocks of Virginia and the world and discusses their uses in daily life.

Admission: Voluntary contribution. Recommended amounts: Adults $4.00/person per day, seniors $3.00, children (12–18) $3.00, children (5–11) $2.00, children under 5 free.

Directions: The museum is located at the corner of U.S. 58 and U.S. 220 in Martinsville.

SECTION 3: Special Events and Tourist Information

TOURIST INFORMATION

State Tourist Agency

Virginia
Phone: (804) 786-2051
Fax: (804) 786-1919
www.VIRGINIA.org

WEST VIRGINIA

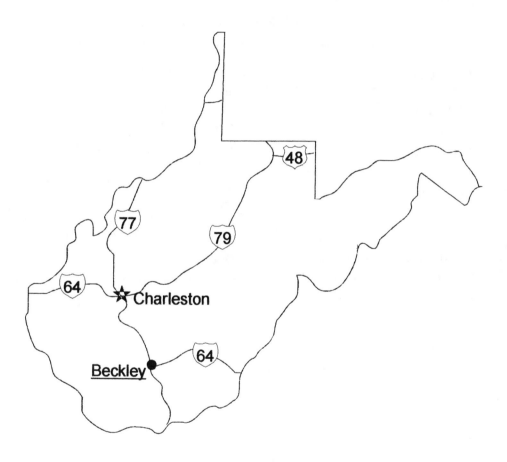

No information available.

BECKLEY

Mine Tour 🏛

The Beckley Exhibition Coal Mine
New River Park
Drawer AJ
Beckley, WV 25802
Phone: (304) 256-1747

Open: April 1–November 1, 10:00 A.M.–6:00 P.M., 7 days/week.

Info: Listed on the National Register of Historical sites, and now part of New River Park, is the restored mine operated by the Phillips family in the late 1800s. Visitors ride a "man trip" car guided through the mine by veteran miners for an authentic view of low seam coal mining from its earliest manual stages to modern mechanized operation. (Bring a jacket—the temperature in the mine is always 58°.)

Visit a company house and a super's (mine superintendent's) house, both of which have been moved to the park and restored. The super's house also has reproductions of the company doctor's offices, the company post office, and the company barbershop. The museum features displays of mining photographs and artifacts from the mining era.

Admission: Adults $8.00, seniors 55+ $7.00, children 4–12 $5.00, children under 4 free.

Other services available: The craft and souvenir shop is open from 10:00 A.M.–6:00 P.M. A 17-site campground at the park provides full hookups.

Directions: From I-77 take exit 44. Turn east on Route 3 (Harper Road). Go 1½ miles to Ewart Avenue, then make a left by Little General. Drive ¼ mile to park entrance.

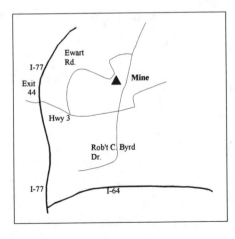

SECTION 3: Special Events and Tourist Information

TOURIST INFORMATION

State Tourist Agency 👉

West Virginia Division of Tourism
2101 Washington Street E.
Charleston, WV 25305
Phone: (800) 225-5982
www.wvweb.com

Index by State

ALABAMA

Fee Dig Mines and Guide Services
    None

Museums and Mine Tours
Anniston   Anniston Museum of Natural History—gemstones, meteorite, artificial indoor cave

ALASKA

Fee Dig Mines and Guide Services
Fairbanks   El Dorado Gold Mine—gold panning
                  Gold Dredge No. 8—gold panning
                  Chena Hot Springs Resort—gold panning

Museums and Mine Tours
Anchorage   Stewart's Photo Shop—gem and mineral displays
Fairbanks   El Dorado Gold Mine—working gold mine tour
                  Gold Dredge No. 8—gold dredge tour
                  University of Alaska Museum—minerals and gems from Alaska, Arctic Canada, and the Pacific Rim; includes gold and meteorites

ARIZONA

Fee Dig Mines and Guide Services
Goldfield   Goldfield Ghost Town, Scenic Railroad, and Mine Tours—gold panning

Museums and Mine Tours
Bisbee   Queen Mine Tour—Tour a copper mine
Flagstaff   Meteor Crater Enterprises, Inc.—View a meteor crater, museum of astrogeology

Goldfield	Goldfield Ghost Town, Scenic Railroad, and Mine Tours—Gold mine tour, museum, ghost town
	Superstition Mountain Museum—Geology, minerals, and mining
Phoenix	Arizona Mining and Mineral Museum—3,000 minerals on exhibit, minerals from AZ copper mines, piece of meteor crater meteorite, rocks from original moon landing, spheres, fluorescent mineral display.
Sun City	The Mineral Museum—3,000 rocks and minerals from the U.S. and the world, with emphasis on minerals from AZ; Over 150 fluorescent rocks and minerals, most from Franklin and Sterling Hill, NJ
Tucson	Arizona-Sonora Desert Museum—Mineral collection from Sonoran desert region
	ASARCO Mineral Discovery Center—Geology, mining, minerals, and tour of open-pit mine
	Mineral Museum, University of Arizona—2,100 of 15,000 minerals on display; AZ minerals, meteorites, fluorescents, borate minerals

Annual Events

Quartzite	Gem & Mineral Shows—mid-January–mid-February
Scottsdale	Minerals of Arizona—Symposium 1 day in March
Tucson	Gem & Mineral Shows—first 2 weeks in February

ARKANSAS

Fee Dig Mines and Guide Services

Glenwood	Crystal Hills Mining Co.—Dig for quartz crystals
Hot Springs	Coleman's Crystal Mine—Dig for quartz crystals
Mt. Ida	Crystal Heaven—Dig for quartz crystals
	Crystal Pyramid—Dig for quartz crystals
	Fiddler's Ridge Rock Shop and Crystal Mines—Dig for quartz crystals
	Leatherhead Quartz Mining—Dig for quartz crystals
	Robbin's Mining Company—Dig for quartz crystals
	Sonny Stanley's Crystal Mine—Dig for quartz crystals
	Starfire Mine—Dig for quartz crystals
	Wegner's Crystal Mine—Dig for quartz crystals
Murfreesboro	Crater of Diamonds State Park—Dig and screen for diamonds, amethyst, agates, barite, calcite, jasper, quartz, other gems

Museums and Mine Tours

Fayetteville   The University Museum—Quartz and other AR minerals
Little Rock   Geology Learning Center—AR gems, minerals, fossil fuels
State University A.S.U. Museum—Minerals, many from AR

Annual Events

Mt. Ida   Quartz Crystal Festival and World Championship Dig—Second weekend in October

CALIFORNIA

Fee Dig Mines and Guide Services

Angels Camp   Jensen's Pick & Shovel Ranch—Guided prospecting for gold
Coloma   Marshall Gold Digging State Historic Park—Gold panning
Columbia   Hidden Treasures Gold Mine Tours—Gold panning
Jackson   Kennedy Gold Mine—Gold panning
Lakeport   Lake County Visitors Information Center—Search for Lake County "diamonds" or "moon tears"
Mariposa   Little Valley Inn—Gold panning
Nevada City   Malakoff Diggins State Historic Park—Gold panning
Palo Verde   Opal Hill Fire Agate Mine—Dig for fire agate, micromount crystals, apatite, barite, calcite, clinoptilolite, fluorite, gypsum (curved)
Pine Grove   Roaring Camp Mining Co.—Pan for gold, rockhounding
Placerville   Gold Bug Mine and Hangtown's Gold Bug Park—Gold panning

Museums and Mine Tours

Allegany   Underground Gold Miners Tours and Museum—Tour an active gold mine
Angels Camp   Angels Camp Museum—Rocks and minerals; gold stamping mill, mining equipment
Avalon   Catalina Island Museum Society Inc.—Exhibits on mining on Catalina Island
Boron   Borax Global Visitors Center—Story of borax
  Boron Twenty Mule Team Museum—History of area borate mining
Coloma   Marshall Gold Discovery State Historic Park—Gold mining exhibit/museum
Columbia   Hidden Treasure Gold Mine—Tour of active gold mine
Death Valley   Furnace Creek Borax Museum—Rocks and minerals, featuring borax minerals

El Cajon	Heritage of the Americas Museum—Rocks, minerals, and meteorites
Fallbrook	Fallbrook Gem & Mineral Museum—Gems and minerals
Grass Valley	Empire Mine State Historic Park—Hardrock gold mine
Jackson	Amador County Museum—Collection of mineral spheres from CA, UT, NV
	Kennedy Gold Mine Tours—Surface tour of gold mine
Julian	Eagle and High Peak Gold Mine Tours—Hardrock gold mine tour
	Julian Pioneer Museum—Rock and mineral display, gold mining tools and equipment displays
Lakeport	Lake County Museum—Minerals and gems from Lake County, CA
Los Angeles	Griffiths Observatory—Display of meteorites
	Natural History Museum of Los Angeles County—52,000 specimens; minerals of CA; native gold, gems, and minerals
Mariposa	California State Mining and Mineral Museum—Gold from CA, gems and minerals from around the world
Needles	Needles Regional Museum—Needles blue agate, Colorado River pebble terrace stones
Nevada City	Malakoff Diggins State Historic Park—History of hydraulic gold mining
Pacific Grove	Pacific Grove Museum of Natural History—Monterey County rocks, fluorescent minerals
Paso Robles	El Paso des Robles Area Pioneer Museum—Display of local minerals
Placerville	Gold Bug Mine and Hangtown's Gold Bug Park—Tour hardrock gold mine
Quincy	Plumas County Museum—Exhibits on silver and copper mining in Plumas County
Rancho Palo Verdes	Point Vicente Interpretive Center—Exhibits on area geology
Redlands	San Bernardino County Museum—45,000 rocks, minerals, and gems
Riverside	Jurupa Mountains Cultural Center—Crestmore minerals display, minerals from around the world on display and for sale, family education programs
	Riverside Municipal Museum—Rocks, minerals, gems, and regional geology
	World Museum of Natural History—Fluorescent minerals, meteorites, tektites, over 1,300 mineral spheres
San Diego	San Diego Natural History Museum—26,000 mineral specimens, includes minerals found in San Diego County mines
Santa Barbara	Department of Geological Sciences, U.C.S.B.—Gem and mineral collection, minerals and their tectonic settings

Shoshone	Shoshone Museum—Rock collection reflecting the geology of the area
Sierra City	Kentucky Mine and Museum—Exhibits of local gold and mercury mining
Sonora	Tuolomne County Museum—Gold from local mines
Yermo	Calico Ghost Town—Explore a silver mine
Yreka	Siskiyou County Courthouse—Gold exhibit
Yucaipa	The Mousley Museum of Natural History—Minerals from famous collection localities around the world
Yucca Valley	Hi-Desert Nature Museum—Rock and mineral collection, includes fluorescent minerals

Annual Events

Boron	Rock Bonanza—weekend before Easter
Coloma	Marshall Gold Discovery State Historic Park: Gold Rush Days—end of September–beginning of October

COLORADO

Fee Dig Mines and Guide Services

Idaho Springs	Argo Gold Mill—Pan for gold and gemstones
	Phoenix Mine—Pan for gold
Lake George (Tarryall)	Topaz Mountain Gem Mine—Screen for topaz, phenakite crystals in topaz, goshenite, quartz, feldspar

Museums and Mine Tours

Denver	Denver Museum of Natural History—2,000 specimens, includes gold, topaz, aquamarine, amazonite, and other Colorado minerals
Georgetown	Lebanon Silver Mine—Tour a silver mine
Golden	Geology Museum, Colorado School of Mines—50,000 specimens, minerals from Colorado and from around the world, gemstones and precious metals, cave exhibit
Idaho Springs	Argo Gold Mill—Historic gold mill, mining museum, Double Eagle Gold Mine
	Edgar Experimental Mine—Tour an experimental mine (silver, gold, lead, copper)
	Phoenix Mine—See a working underground hardrock mine (gold, silver)
Leadville	Matchless Mine—Tour a gold mine
	National Mining Hall of Fame and Museum—Story of the American mining industry from coal to gold.

Silverton   Mayflower Gold Mill—Tour a gold mill

Old Hundred Gold Mine Tour, Inc.—Gold mine tour

San Juan County Historical Museum—Minerals and gems from the Silverton area

CONNECTICUT

Fee Dig Mines and Guide Services

None

Museums and Mine Tours

East Granby   Old New-Gate Prison and Copper Mine—Tour an old copper mine

Greenwich   Bruce Museum of Arts and Science—Minerals and rocks

New Haven   Peabody Museum of Natural History—Minerals of New England and the world

DELAWARE

Fee Dig Mines and Guide Services

None

Museums and Mine Tours

Newark   Delaware Academy of Science, Iron Hill Museum—DE minerals, fluorescent minerals

University of Delaware, Mineralogical Museum—5,000 specimens (1,000 on display), crystals, gems, minerals

DISTRICT OF COLUMBIA

Fee Dig Mines and Guide Services

None

Museums and Mine Tours

Smithsonian Institution, National Museum of Natural History—Gems and minerals

FLORIDA

Fee Dig Mines and Guide Services

None

Museums and Mine Tours

Mulberry   Mulberry Phosphate Museum—Exhibits on the phosphate industry

Tampa   Ed and Bernadette Marcin Museum, University of Florida—Minerals and gemstones mainly from FL and the western U.S.

GEORGIA

Fee Dig Mines and Guide Services

Dahlonega   Consolidated Gold Mine—Gold panning

                 Crisson Gold Mine—Pan gold sands or enriched gemstone ore

Helen   Gold Mine of Helen, GA—Pan gold sand or enriched gemstone ore

Museums and Mine Tours

Cartersville William Weinman Mineral Museum—2,000 specimens, gems and minerals from the state; simulated cave

Dahlonega   Consolidated Gold Mine—Mine tour

                 Dahlonega Gold Museum—Tells the story of the GA Gold Rush

Elberton   Elberton Granite Museum—Granite quarry and products

Helen   Gold Mine of Helen, GA—Mine tour

Statesboro   Georgia Southern Museum—Collection of rocks and minerals from Georgia's highlands, piedmont, and coastal regions

Annual Events

Jasper   Pickens County Marble Festival—first weekend in October

HAWAII

Fee Dig Mines and Guide Services

                 None

Museums and Mine Tours

**Hawaii Nat'l   Thomas A. Jaggar Museum—Museum on vulcanology and seismol-
Park**   ogy; tour of volcano

Hilo   Lyman House Memorial Museum—Rocks, minerals, gems

IDAHO

Fee Dig Mines and Guide Services

Moscow   3-D's Panhandle Gems and Garnet Queen Mine—Guide service, star garnet digging; trips including gold panning.

| Spencer | Spencer Opal Mine—Pick through a stockpile for fire opal; pre-arranged digging at mine is a possibility |
| St. Maries | Emerald Creek Garnet Area—Dig for star garnets |

Museums and Mine Tours

| Caldwell | The Glen L. and Ruth M. Evans Gem and Mineral Collection—Agate, jasper, other gemstones, 2,000 cabochons |
| | Orma J. Smith Museum of Natural History—Extensive collection of minerals |

ILLINOIS

Fee Dig Mines and Guide Services
None

Museums and Mine Tours

Chicago	The Field Museum—92-year-old gem exhibit
Elmhurst	Lizzandro Museum of Lapidary Art—1,300 pieces of cut and polished gems, fluorescent rocks, a birthstone display
Galena	Vinegar Hill Lead Mine and Museum—Mine tour and museum
Springfield	Illinois State Museum—Gems and minerals, Illinois specimens, birthstones, fluorescents, copper
Urbana	Museum of Natural History—Rocks, minerals, meteorites
West Frankfort	The National Coal Museum, Mine 25—Tour a shaft coal mine

INDIANA

Fee Dig Mines and Guide Services

| Knightstown | Yogi Bear Jellystone Park Camping Resort—Midwestern gold prospecting |

Museums and Mine Tours

Bedford	Land of Limestone Exhibition—History of Indiana Limestone industry
Indianapolis	Indiana State Museum—Indiana and regional minerals
Richmond	Joseph Moore Museum of Natural History, Earlham College—Geology exhibit from local Ordovician limestone

IOWA

Fee Dig Mines and Guide Services
Bonaport   Butch Lewis Guide Services—Geodes

Museums and Mine Tours
Danville   Geode State Park—Display of geodes
Forest City Timberland Museum—Rocks, minerals, semiprecious stones, meteorite fragments
Iowa City   University of Iowa—Displays on state geology
Sioux City   Sioux City Public Museum—Mineralogy exhibit
Waterloo   Grout Museum—Display of rocks and minerals
West Bend   Grotto of the Redemption—Grotto made of precious stones and gems
Winterset   Madison County Historical Society—Rock and mineral collection

KANSAS

Fee Dig Mines and Guide Services
None

Museums and Mine Tours
Greensburg   Pallasite Meteorite at the Big Well Museum—Meteorite strike site and 1,000-pound meteorite
McPherson   McPherson Museum—Meteorites

KENTUCKY

Fee Dig Mines and Guide Services
None

Museums and Mine Tours
Benham   Kentucky Coal Mine Museum—Displays on coal mining and formation of coal
Lynch   Lynch Portal 31 Walking Tour—Walking tour of coal mining facilities

LOUISIANA

Fee Dig Mines and Guide Services
None

Museums and Mine Tours

New Orleans   Louisiana Nature Center—Small collection of gems and minerals

Shreveport   Louisiana State Exhibit Museum—Displays on mining and salt domes

MAINE

Fee Dig Mines and Guide Services

Bethel   Songo Pond Mine—Collect tourmaline and other ME gems and minerals

Poland   Poland Mining Camp—Collect tourmaline and other ME gems and minerals

West Paris   Perham's of West Paris—Collect tourmaline and other ME gems and minerals

Museums and Mine Tours

Augusta   Maine State Museum—Gems and minerals of ME

West Paris   Perham's of West Paris—ME gems and minerals; model of a feldspar quarry, model of a gem tourmaline pocket, fluorescents

Annual Events

Augusta   Maine Mineral Symposium—3rd weekend in May

MARYLAND

Fee Dig Mines and Guide Services
None

Museums and Mine Tours
None

MASSACHUSETTS

Fee Dig Mines and Guide Services

Athol   Richards Gold Mine—Gold panning trip to a mine located in VT

Museums and Mine Tours

Amherst   Pratt Museum of Natural History—10,000 specimens; minerals from New England and round the world, meteorites

Cambridge   Harvard University Museum of Cultural and Natural History—Gems, minerals, ores, meteorites

MICHIGAN

Fee Dig Mines and Guide Services
Kearsarge   Delaware Copper Mine—Search for souvenir copper

Museums and Mine Tours
Ann Arbor   Exhibit Museum of Natural History, University of Michigan—Exhibits of rocks and minerals

Bloomfield Hills Cranbrook Institute of Science—5,000 minerals and crystals from around the world, including hiddenite, gold

Calumet   Mining Museum at Coppertown, U.S.A.—Exhibits on copper mining

Caspian   Iron County Museum and Park—Iron mining complex

Chelsea   Gerald E. Eddy Geology Center—Michigan rocks, minerals, crystals, and mining

Copper Harbor Fort Wilkins State Park—History of copper mining in the area

Grand Rapids   Michigan Natural Storage Co.—Tour an underground gypsum mine

Hancock   The Quincy Mining Company—Tour an underground copper mine

Houghton   The Seaman Mineral Museum—Crystal collection, minerals from the Lake Superior copper district

Iron Mountain Iron Mountain Iron Mine—Iron mine tour

Kearsarge   Delaware Copper Mine—Mine tour

Lake Linden   Houghton County Historical Museum—Copper mining and refining equipment displays

Mount Pleasant Museum of Cultural and Natural History, Central Michigan University—MI rocks and minerals

Negaunee   Michigan Iron Industry Museum—Story of MI iron industry

Shelby   Shelby Man—Made Gemstones—Exhibits on producing artificial gems

MINNESOTA

Fee Dig Mines and Guide Services
            None

Museums and Mine Tours
Calumet   Hill Annex Mine State Park—Tour an open pit iron mine

Chisholm   Ironworld Discovery Center—Iron industry taconite mining tours
            Minnesota Museum of Mining—Indoor and outdoor exhibits
            Taconite Mine Tours—Tour of an open-pit iron ore mine

Hibbing	Mahoning Hull-Rust Mine—Observe an open-pit iron mine
Pipestone	Pipestone National Monument—Tour a Native American pipestone quarry
Soudan	Soudan Underground Mine State Park—Tour an underground iron mine
Virginia	Mineview in the Sky—View an open-pit iron ore mine
	Iron Trails Conventions and Visitor's Bureau—Information on mine view sites

MISSISSIPPI

Fee Dig Mines and Guide Services
> None

Museums and Mine Tours

Greenwood Cottonlandia Museum—Rocks and minerals from around the world

MISSOURI

Fee Dig Mines and Guide Services

Alexandria Sheffler Rock Shop—Dig geodes lined with crystals

Revere Geode Hollow Rock Shop and Mine—Dig geodes lined with crystals

Museums and Mine Tours

Golden Golden Pioneer Museum—Large mineral exhibit

Joplin Everett J. Richie Tri-State Mineral Museum—Story of area's lead and zinc mining

Park Hills Missouri Mines State Historic Site—1,100 minerals, ores, and rocks

Point Lookout Ralph Foster Museum, College of the Ozarks—Gemstone spheres and fluorescent minerals

Rolla Mineral Museum, U. of Missouri, Rolla—3,500 minerals, ores, and rocks from 92 countries and 47 states

MONTANA

Fee Dig Mines and Guide Services

Alder Red Rock Mine—Screen for garnets

Clinton L◊E Guest Ranch Outfitters—Sapphire mining pack trips

Dillon Crystal Park Recreational Mineral Collecting Area—Dig for quartz and amethyst crystal

Helena El Dorado Sapphire Mines—Dig and screen for sapphires

Spokane	Spokane Bar Sapphire Mine and Gold Fever Rock Shop—Dig and screen for sapphires and other gems and minerals
Phillipsburg	Sapphire Gallery—Wash bags of gravel to look for sapphires.

Museums and Mine Tours

Butte	Anselmo Mine Yard—Tour of mining facilities and history of area mining
	The Berkeley Pit—Observation point for closed open-pit copper mine
	Butte-Silver Bow Visitors and Transportation Center—Presents information on area geology and its mining, including local gold and silver mining
	Mineral Museum, Montana College of Mineral Science and Technology—Gold, fluorescents, and minerals from Butte and MT
	World Museum of Mining and 1899 Mining Camp—Tour of surface facilities of former silver and zinc mine
Lewistown	Central Montana Museum—Rocks, minerals, and yogo sapphires

NEBRASKA

Fee Dig Mines and Guide Services

None

Museums and Mine Tours

Hastings	Hastings Museum—Minerals, rocks, fluorescent minerals, and translucent slabs
Lincoln	University of Nebraska State Museum—Displays of rocks, minerals and fluorescent rocks

NEVADA

Fee Dig Mines and Guide Services

Denio	Rainbow Ridge Opal Mine—Tailings digging for wood opal
Ely	Garnet Fields Rockhound Area—Hunt for garnets
Gerlach	Royal Rainbow Fire Opal Mine—Dig for fire opal
Orovado	Royal Peacock Opal Mine, Inc.—Dig black and fire opal
Sun Valley	American Gem Tours—Turquoise, blue chalcedony, precious opal, Oregon sunstone

Museums and Mine Tours

Carson City	Nevada State Museum—Nevada geological history and replica of NV mine

Virginia City   Chollar Mine—Underground mine tour (gold and silver mine)

NEW HAMPSHIRE

Fee Dig Mines and Guide Services
Grafton   Ruggles Mine—Collect up to 150 different minerals

Museums and Mine Tours
Dover   The Woodman Institute—1,300 specimens, including local rocks

NEW JERSEY

Fee Dig Mines and Guide Services
Cape May   Cape May Welcome Center—Hunt for Cape May "diamonds"
Franklin   Franklin Mineral Museum and Buckwheat Dump—Tailings diggings for fluorescent minerals

Museums and Mine Tours
Franklin   Franklin Mineral Museum—Minerals, rocks, local and worldwide fluorescents
Jamesburg   Displayworld's Stone Museum—Minerals, hands-on exhibits
New Brunswick Rutgers Geology Museum—Specimens from the zinc deposit at Franklin and the zeolite deposits from Paterson, meteorites
Ogdensburg   Sterling Hill Mine and Museum—Tour old zinc mine
Paterson   The Paterson Museum—Specimens from local basalt flows and basalt flow in the Poona region of India, minerals from NJ and around the world
Rutherford   Meadowland Museum—Fluorescent minerals, quartz, minerals from NJ
Trenton   New Jersey State Museum—Minerals and rocks, including fluorescents and magnetite ore

Annual Events
Franklin   New Jersey Earth Science Association Gem and Mineral Show and Outdoor Swap & Sell—Late April

NEW MEXICO

Fee Dig Mines and Guide Services
Bingham   Blanchard Mines—Collect over 84 different kinds of minerals in a former lead mine
Deming   Rockhound State Park—collect a variety of semiprecious stones

| Dixon | Harding Mine—Harding pegmatite has yielded over 50 minerals |
| Magdalena | Bill's Gems & Minerals—Collect copper and iron minerals at mine dumps |

Museums and Mine Tours

Albuquerque	Institute of Meteoritics, University of New Mexico—Meteorites
	New Mexico Museum of Natural History and Science—3,000 specimens with a focus on New Mexico and the southwestern U.S.
	The Turquoise Museum—Turquoise museum
Socorro	New Mexico Bureau of Mines and Mineral Resources—10,000 specimens of minerals from NM, the U.S., and the world

Annual Events

| Socorro | Rockhounding Days in Socorro County—last weekend in March |

NEW YORK

Fee Dig Mines and Guide Services

Herkimer	Herkimer Diamond Mine and KOA Kampground—Dig for Herkimer "Diamonds"
Middleville	Ace of Diamonds Mine and Campground—Prospect for Herkimer "Diamonds"
St. Johnsville	Crystal Grove Diamond Mine and Campground—Dig for Herkimer "Diamonds"

Museums and Mine Tours

Hicksville	The Hicksville Gregory Museum—9,000 specimens form the major minerals groups; also NJ zeolites, Herkimer "diamonds," fluorescents
New York	American Museum of Natural History—Gems, meteorites; emphasis on exceptional specimens from the U.S.
Pawling	The Gunnison Natural History Museum—Minerals

NORTH CAROLINA

Fee Dig Mines and Guide Services

Almond	Nantahala Gorge Ruby Mine—Sluice for rubies, sapphires, amethyst, topaz, garnet, citrine, smoky quartz
Canton	Old Pressley Sapphire Mine—Sluice for sapphires
Cherokee	Smoky Mountain Gold & Ruby Mine—Sluice for gold and gems
Franklin	Cherokee Ruby and Sapphire Mine—Sluice for rubies, sapphires, garnets, moonstones, rutile, sillimanite

Cowee Valley Ruby Mine—Sluice for rubies, sapphires, garnets, tourmaline, smoky quartz, amethyst, citrine, moonstone, topaz

Gem City Mine—Sluice for rubies, sapphires, garnets, tourmaline, smoky quartz, amethyst, citrine, moonstone, topaz

Gold City Gem Mine—Sluice for rubies, sapphires, garnets, emeralds, tourmaline, smoky quartz, amethyst, citrine, moonstone, topaz

Jackson Hole—Sluice for rubies, sapphire, garnets, tourmaline, smoky quartz, amethyst, citrine, moonstone, topaz

Jacobs Ruby Mine—Sluice for rubies, sapphire, rhodolite, garnets, other precious stones

Mason Mountain Rhodolite and Ruby Mine and Cowee Gift Shop—Sluice for rhodolite, rubies, sapphires, garnets, kyanite, crystal quartz, smoky quartz, moonstones

Masons Ruby and Sapphire Mine—Dig and sluice for sapphires (all colors), pink and red rubies

Moonstone Gem Mine—Sluice for rhodolite, rubies, sapphires, garnets, other precious stones

The Old Cardinal Gem Mine—Sluice for rare native rhodolite, rubies, sapphires, garnets, moonstones, topaz, other precious stones

Rocky Face Gem Mine—Sluice for rubies, rhodolite garnets

Rose Creek Mine, Campground, Trout Pond, and Rock Shop—Sluice for rubies, sapphires, garnets, moonstones, amethysts, smoky quartz, citrine, rose quartz, topaz

Sheffield Mine—Sluice for rubies, sapphires, enriched material from around the world

Hiddenite   Emerald Hollow Mine, Hiddenite Gems, Inc.—Rutile, sapphires, garnets, monazite, hiddenite, smoky quartz, tourmaline, clear quartz, aquamarine, sillimanite

**Little
Switzerland**   Blue Ridge Gemstone Mine & Campground—Sapphire, emeralds, rubies, aquamarine, tourmaline, topaz, garnets, amethysts, lepidolite, citrine, moonstone, kyanite, and rose, clear, rutilated, and smoky quartz

Emerald Village—Sapphire, emeralds, rubies, aquamarine, tourmaline, topaz, garnets, amethysts, lepidolite, citrine, beryl, moonstone, kyanite, and rose, clear, rutilated, and smoky quartz

Marion   The Lucky Strike—Gems and gold panning

New London   Cotton Patch Gold Mine—Gold panning

Spruce Pine   Gem Mountain Gemstone Mine—Sapphires, crabtree emeralds, rubies, Wiseman aquamarine

Rio Doce Gem Mine—Sapphires, emeralds, rubies, aquamarine,

tourmaline, topaz, garnets, amethysts, lepidolite, citrine, beryl, moonstone, kyanite, and rose, clear, rutilated, and smoky quartz

Spruce Pine Gem and Gold Mine—Sapphires, emeralds, rubies, aquamarine, tourmaline, topaz, garnets, amethysts, lepidolite, citrine, beryl, moonstone, kyanite, and rose, clear, rutilated, and smoky quartz

Stanfield   Reed Gold Mine Historic Site—Gold panning

Union Mills   Thermal City Gold Mining Company—Gold panning

Museums and Mine Tours

Asheville   Colburn Gem & Mineral Museum—Collection of mineral specimens from NC and the world

Franklin   Franklin Gem and Mineral Museum—Specimens from NC and around the world

Ruby City Gems—Specimens from NC and around the world

Greensboro   Natural Science Center of Greensboro—Specimens from NC and around the world

Hendersonville Mineral and Lapidary Museum of Hendersonville, Inc.—Minerals and lapidary arts

Linville   Grandfather Mountain Nature Museum—Specimens from NC

Little Switzerland North Carolina Mining Museum and Mine Tour—tour a closed feldspar mine

Spruce Pine   Museum of North Carolina Minerals—Specimens primarily from local mines

Stanfield   Reed Gold Mine Historic Site—Gold mine tour

Annual Events

Franklin   Macon County Gemboree—3rd weekend in July

"Leaf Looker" Gemboree—2nd weekend in October

Spruce Pine   Original NC Mineral and Gem Festival—4 days at the beginning of August

NORTH DAKOTA

Fee Dig Mines and Guide Services

None

Museums and Mine Tours

Dickinson   Dakota Dinosaur Museum—Rocks and minerals, including borax from CA, turquoise from AZ, fluorescents, aurora crystals from AR

OHIO

Fee Dig Mines and Guide Services
Hopewell   Hidden Springs Ranch—Dig for flint (groups only)
Nethers Flint—Dig for flint

Museums and Mine Tours
Brownsville Flint Ridge State Memorial—Ancient flint quarrying
Cleveland   The Cleveland Museum of Natural History—The Wade Gallery of Gems and Minerals has over 1,500 gems and minerals
Columbus   Orton Geological Museum—Rocks and minerals from OH and the world
Dayton   Boonshoft Museum of Discovery—Minerals and crystals
Lima   Allen County Museum—Rock and mineral exhibit

OKLAHOMA

Fee Dig Mines and Guide Services
Jet   Salt Plains National Wildlife Refuge—Digging for selenite crystals
Kenton   Black Mesa Bed & Breakfast—Rockhounding on a working cattle ranch
Howard Layton Ranch—Rockhounding on a working cattle ranch

Museums and Mine Tours
Coalgate   Coal Country Mining and Historical Museum—Mining museum
Enid   The Mr. and Mrs. Dan Midgley Museum—Rock and mineral collection predominantly from OK and the TX shoreline
Noble   Timberlake Rose Rock Museum—Displays of barite roses
Picher   Picher Mining Museum—Lead and zinc mining
Tulsa   Elsing Museum—Gems and minerals

Annual Events
Cherokee   The Crystal Festival and Selenite Crystal Dig—First Saturday in May
Noble   Annual Rose Rock Festival—First Saturday in May

OREGON

Fee Dig Mines and Guide Services
Madras   Richards Recreational Ranch—Dig for thundereggs, agate
Mitchell   Lucky Strike Geodes—Dig for thundereggs (picture jasper)
Yachats   Beachcombing—Collect agates and jaspers

Museums and Mine Tours

Central Point	Crater Rock Museum—Minerals, thundereggs, fossils, geodes, cut and polished gemstones
Redmond	Peterson's Rock Garden—Unusual rock specimens, fluorescent display
Sumpter	Sumpter Valley Dredge State Historical Heritage Area—View a gold dredge, tour historic gold mine towns

Annual Events

Cottage Grove	Bohemia Mining Days—Four days in July, gold panning and exposition
Prineville	Rockhounds Pow-Wow—mid-June

PENNSYLVANIA

Fee Dig Mines and Guide Services

> None

Museums and Mine Tours

Ashland	Museum of Anthracite Mining—Story of anthracite coal
	Pioneer Tunnel Coal Mine—Tour an anthracite coal mine
Bryn Mawr	Museum, Department of Geology, Bryn Mawr College—Rotating display of 1,500 minerals from collection of 23,500 specimens
Harrisburg	State Museum of Pennsylvania—Geology of everyday products
Lancaster	North Museum of Natural History and Science—Worldwide specimens with a focus on Lancaster County
Media	Delaware County Institute of Science—Minerals from around the world
Philadelphia	Wagner Free Institute of Science—Rocks and minerals
Pittsburgh	Carnegie Museum of Natural History—Gems and minerals
Scranton	Anthracite Museum Complex—Several anthracite coal–related attractions, including mine tours and museums
St. Boniface	Seldom Seen Mine—Tour a bituminous coal mine
Tarentum	Tour-Ed Mine—Bituminous coal mine tour
University Park	College of Earth and Mineral Sciences, Penn State University—Minerals
Waynesburg	Paul R. Stewart Museum, Waynesburg College—Outstanding mineral collection
West Chester	Geology Museum, West Chester University—Specimens from Chester County, fluorescent specimens
Wilkes-Barre	Wyoming Historical & Geological Society Museum—Displays on anthracite coal mining

Annual Events

Pittsburgh The Carnegie Museum of Natural History Gem & Mineral Show—last weekend in August

University Park Mineral Symposium—Three days in May

RHODE ISLAND

Fee Dig Mines and Guide Services
> None

Museums and Mine Tours

Providence Museum of Natural History and Planetarium—Rocks and minerals

SOUTH CAROLINA

Fee Dig Mines and Guide Services
> None

Museums and Mine Tours

Charleston Charleston Museum—Small display of gems and minerals

Clemson Bob Campbell Geology Museum—Minerals, meteorites, faceted stones

Columbia McKissick Museum, University of South Carolina Campus—Exhibits on geology and gemstones

South Carolina State Museum—Small display of rocks and minerals

SOUTH DAKOTA

Fee Dig Mines and Guide Services

Custer Tom Breen—Guide Service—Collect feldspar, quartz, and others

Deadwood Broken Boot Gold Mine—Pan for gold

Keystone Big Thunder Gold Mine—Pan for gold

Lead Black Hills Mining Museum—Pan for gold

Wall Buffalo Gap National Grasslands—Hunt for agates

Museums and Mine Tours

Deadwood Broken Boot Gold Mine—Gold mine tour

Keystone Big Thunder Gold Mine—Underground mine tour

Lead Black Hills Mining Museum—Simulated underground mine tour

Homestead Visitors Center—Gold mining displays

Murdo	National Rockhound and Lapidary Hall of Fame—Gems and minerals
Rapid City	South Dakota School of Mines and Technology—Local minerals

TENNESSEE

Fee Dig Mines and Guide Services
None

Museums and Mine Tours
Johnson City	Hands On! Regional Museum—Simulated coal mine
Memphis	Memphis Pink Palace Museum—Geology and minerals from famous mid-South localities.

TEXAS

Fee Dig Mines and Guide Services
Alpine	Stillwell Ranch—Hunt for agate and jasper
	Woodward Ranch—Hunt for agate, precious opal, and others
Mason	Hoffman Ranch—Hunt for topaz
	Seaquist Ranch—Hunt for topaz
Three Rivers	House Ranch—Hunt for agate

Museums and Mine Tours
Austin	Texas Memorial Museum—Gems and minerals
Canyon	Panhandle Plains Historical Museum—Gems and minerals from the TX panhandle; meteorites
Fritch	Alibates Flint Quarries—View ancient flint quarries
Marble Falls	Granite Mountain—View marble mining operations
McKinney	The Heard Natural Science Museum and Wildlife Sanctuary—Rocks and minerals
Odessa	Odessa Meteor Crater—Meteorite crater

Annual Events
Alpine	Alpine Gem Show—mid-April

UTAH

Fee Dig Mines and Guide Services
Moab	Lin Ottinger's Tours—Guide services: Collect crystals, agates, azurite, malachite

Museums and Mine Tours

Eureka   Tintec Mining Museum—Mineral display and mining artifacts
Helper   Western Mining and Railroad Museum—Mining exhibits, simulated 1900 coal mine
Hyrum   Hyrum City Museum—Display of fluorescent minerals
Lehi   John Hutchings Museum of Natural History—Minerals linked to mining districts, display of uncut gems
Magna   Bingham Canyon Mine Visitors Center—Overlook for open-pit copper mine
Salt Lake City Utah Museum of Natural History—Mineral classification; UT ores and minerals, fluorescent minerals

VERMONT

Fee Dig Mines and Guide Services
None (See Athol, MA)

Museums and Mine Tours

Barre   Rock of Ages Corporation—Watch granite being quarried
Norwich   Montshire Museum of Science—Fluorescent minerals
Proctor   Vermont Marble Exhibit—Story of marble

VIRGINIA

Fee Dig Mines and Guide Services

Amelia   Dick R. Boyles—Dig for beryl
                  Morefield Gem Mine—Dig and sluice for garnet, quartz, topaz, and many others
Stuart   Fairy Stone State Park—Hunt for staurolite crystals (fairy stones)

Museums and Mine Tours

Martinsville Virginia Museum of Natural History—Minerals and mining exhibits

WASHINGTON

Fee Dig Mines and Guide Services

Ravensdale   Bob Jackson's Geology Adventures—Field trips: collect quartz, garnets, topaz, and others

Museums and Mine Tours

Castle Rock   Mount St. Helens National Volcanic Monument—Focus on geology

Ellensburg	Kittitas County Historical Museum and Society—Polished rocks
Pullman	Washington State University—Silicified wood, minerals
Seattle	Burke Museum of Natural History and Culture—Rocks, minerals, the geology of Washington, and a walk-through volcano

WEST VIRGINIA

Fee Dig Mines and Guide Services
None

Museums and Mine Tours
| Beckley | The Beckley Exhibition Coal Mine—Tour a bituminous coal mine |

WISCONSIN

Fee Dig Mines and Guide Services
None

Museums and Mine Tours
Dodgeville	The Museum of Minerals and Crystals—Local mineral specimens, specimens from around the world
Hurley	Iron County Historical Museum—History of area mining, also, last remaining mine head frame in Wisconsin
Madison	Geology Museum, University of Wisconsin at Madison—Minerals, fluorescent minerals, model of Wisconsin cave
Milwaukee	Milwaukee Public Museum—Displays of geological specimens
	University of Wisconsin at Milwaukee—Minerals
Platteville	The Mining Museum—Lead and zinc mining in the upper Mississippi Valley
Stevens Point	Museum of Natural History—University of Wisconsin—Stevens Point rock and mineral display

WYOMING

Fee Dig Mines and Guide Services
| Shell | Trapper Galloway Ranch—Dig for moss agate |

Museums and Mine Tours
| Casper | Tate Geological Museum—Rocks and minerals, including WY jade, and fluorescent minerals |
| Laramie | Geological Museum, University of Wyoming—Rocks and minerals, fluorescent minerals from WY |

| **Saritoga** | Saritoga Museum—Minerals from around the world, local geology |
| **Worland** | Washaki Museum—Agates, crystals |

Annual Events

| **Casper** | Tate Geological Museum Symposium on Wyoming Geology—June |

Index by Gems and Minerals

This index lists all the gems and minerals that can be found at fee dig mines in the U.S., and shows the city and state where the mine is located. To use the index, look up the gem or mineral you are interested in, and note the states and cities where they are located. Then go to the state and city to find the name of the mine, and information about the mine.

The following notes provide additional information:

(#)   A number in parentheses is the number of mines in that town that have that gem or mineral.

(*)   Gem or mineral is found in the state, but the mine may also add material to the ore. Check with the individual mine for confirmation.

(FT)   Field trip.

(GS)   Guide service (location listed is the location of the guide service, not necessarily the location of the gems or minerals being collected).

(I)   Mineral has been identified at the mine site but may be difficult to find.

(M)   Museum that allows collection of one specimen as a souvenir.

(MM)   Micromount (a very small crystal which, when viewed under a microscope or magnifying glass, is found to be a high-quality crystal).

(O)   Available at mine but comes from other mines.

(R)   Can be found, but is rare.

(S)   Not the main gem or mineral for which the site is known.

(SA)   "Salted" or enriched gem or mineral.

(U)   Unique to the site.

(Y)   Yearly collecting event.

Agate Arkansas: Murfreesboro (S); Iowa: Bonaporte; Montana: Helena (S); Nevada: Gerlach; New Mexico: Deming (GS); Oklahoma: Kenton (2); Oregon: Yachats; South Dakota: Wall; Texas: Three Rivers; Utah: Moab (GS); Virginia: Amelia

Banded agate Texas: Alpine
Fire agate California: Palo Verde
Iris agate Texas: Alpine
Ledge agate Oregon: Madras
Moss agate Oregon: Madras, Mitchell; Texas: Alpine (2); Wyoming: Shell
Polka-dot jasp-agate Oregon: Madras
Plume agate Oregon: Madras
Pompom agate Texas: Alpine
Rainbow agate Oregon: Madras
Red plume agate Texas: Alpine

Albite Maine: Poland (GS), West Paris; New Hampshire: Grafton (I); New Mexico: Dixon

Albite (Cleavelandite Var.) Maine: Poland (GS)

Amazonite Virginia: Amelia

Amber Texas: Mason (R); Washington: Ravensdale (GS)

Amethyst Arkansas: Murfreesboro (S); Georgia: Helen (SA); Maine: Bethel (R), West Paris; Montana: Dillon; New Hampshire: Grafton (I); New Mexico: Bingham; North Carolina (*): Almond, Cherokee, Franklin (5), Little Switzerland, Spruce Pine (3)
Crystal scepters Nevada: Sun Valley (GS)

Amblygonite Maine: West Paris

Amphibolite New Hampshire: Grafton (I)

Apatite California: Palo Verde (MM); Maine: Bethel, Poland (GS), West Paris; New Hampshire: Grafton; New Mexico, Dixon
Fluorapatite Maine: Poland (GS)
Green apatite Maine: West Paris
Hydroxylapatite Maine: Poland (GS)
Purple apatite Maine: West Paris

Aplite New Hampshire: Grafton (I)

Aquamarine Maine: Bethel, Poland (GS); New Hampshire: Grafton (I); North Carolina (*): Hiddenite, Little Switzerland (2), Spruce Pine (2) (FT)
Brushy Creek aquamarine North Carolina: Spruce Pine (1) (FT)
Weisman aquamarine North Carolina: Spruce Pine (1) (FT)

Arsenopyrite Maine: Poland (GS)

Augelite Maine: Poland (GS)

Aurichalcite New Mexico: Bingham, Magdalena

Autenite Maine: Poland (GS); New Hampshire: Grafton (I)

Azurite New Mexico: Magdalena; Utah: Moab (GS)

Barite Arkansas: Murfreesboro (S); California: Palo Verde (MM); New Mexico: Bingham; Washington: Ravensdale (GS)

Beraumite Maine: Poland (GS)

Bermanite Maine: Poland (GS)

Bertrandite Maine: Poland (GS), West Paris

Bertranite New Hampshire: Grafton (I)

Beryl Maine: Poland (GS), West Paris; New Mexico, Dixon; North Carolina (*): Little Switzerland (2), Spruce Pine (2); South Dakota: Custer (GS); Virginia: Amelia (2)

    Aqua beryl New Hampshire: Grafton (I)

    Blue beryl (see also aquamarine) New Hampshire: Grafton (I)

    Golden beryl North Carolina: Spruce Pine (FT); New Hampshire: Grafton (I)

Beryllonite Maine: Poland (GS), West Paris

Biotite New Hampshire: Grafton (I)

Borate California: Boron (Y)

Bornite New Hampshire: Grafton (I)

Brazilianite Maine: Poland (GS)

Brochantite New Mexico: Bingham

Calcite Arkansas: Murfreesboro (S); California: Palo Verde (MM); New Hampshire: Grafton; New Mexico: Bingham; Virginia: Amelia

Cape May "diamonds" See Quartz

Casserite Maine: Poland (GS)

Cassiterite Maine: West Paris

Cerussite New Mexico: Bingham

Chalcedony New Mexico: Deming

Chalcedony, Blue Nevada: Sun Valley (GS)

Childrenite Maine: Poland (GS)

Chrysoberyl Maine: West Paris; New Hampshire: Grafton (I)

Chrysocolla New Mexico: Bingham

Citrine Georgia: Helen (SA); North Carolina (SA): Almond, Cherokee, Franklin (6), Little Switzerland, Spruce Pine (3)

Clarkite New Hampshire: Grafton (I)

Clevelandite Maine: West Paris; New Hampshire: Grafton (I); New Mexico: Dixon

Clinoptilolite California: Palo Verde (MM)

Columbite New Hampshire: Grafton (I); Maine: Bethel, Poland (GS), West Paris

Compotite New Hampshire: Grafton (I)

Cookeite Maine: West Paris

Copper minerals Michigan: Kearsage (M); New Mexico: Magdalena

Covellite New Mexico: Bingham

Cryolite New Hampshire: Grafton (I)

Cuprite New Mexico: Bingham

Cymatolite New Hampshire: Grafton (I)

Dendrites Nevada: Gerlach; New Hampshire: Grafton (I)

Diadochite Maine: Poland (GS)

Diamond Arkansas: Murfreesboro

Dickinsonite Maine: Poland (GS)

Earlshannonite Maine: Poland (GS)

Elbaite See listing under Tourmaline

Emerald Georgia: Dahlonega (SA); North Carolina (*): Cherokee, Franklin, Hiddenite, Little Switzerland (2), Spruce Pine (2)
  Crabtree Emerald North Carolina: Spruce Pine

Eosphorite Maine: Poland (GS)

Fairfieldite Maine: Poland (GS)

Fairy stones (See Staurolite crystals)

Feldspar Colorado: Lake George; New Hampshire: Grafton (I); South Dakota: Custer (GS); Virginia: Amelia
  Albite feldspar Maine: Bethel

Flint Ohio: Hopewell (2)

Fluoroapatite New Hampshire: Grafton (I)

Fluorescent minerals New Jersey: Franklin; North Carolina: Little Switzerland; Washington: Ravensdale (GS)

Fluorite California: Palo Verde (MM); New Mexico: Bingham, Socorro (Y); South Dakota: Custer (GS); Virginia: Amelia; Washington: Ravensdale (GS)

Gahnite (spinel) Maine: Poland (GS), West Paris

Gainsite Maine: Poland (GS)

Galena New Mexico: Bingham

Garnets Georgia: Dahlonega (SA), Helen (SA); Idaho: St. Maries; Maine: Bethel, Poland (GS), West Paris (3); Montana: Alder, Helena (S); New Hampshire: Grafton (I); New Mexico: Dixon; North Carolina (*): Almond, Cherokee, Franklin (7), Hiddenite, Little Switzerland (2), Spruce Pine (3) (FT); Nevada: Ely; Washington: Ravensdale (GS)
  Almandine garnets Maine: Poland (GS); Nevada, Ely
  Pyrope garnets North Carolina: Franklin
  Rhodolite garnets North Carolina: Franklin (5)

Garnets, Star Idaho: Moscow (GS), St. Maries

Geodes Iowa: Bonaporte (GS); Missouri: Alexandria, Revere; New Mexico: Deming

Lined with:

Agate, blue New Mexico: Deming

Aragonite Missouri: Alexandria

Barites Missouri: Alexandria

Brown calcite crystals Missouri: Revere

Calcite Missouri: Alexandria, Revere

Chalcedony New Mexico; Deming

Dew-drop diamonds Missouri: Revere

Dolomite Missouri: Alexandria

Fluoresdite crystals Missouri: Revere

Goethite Missouri: Alexandria

Hematite Missouri: Alexandria

Kaoline Missouri: Alexandria

Opal, common New Mexico: Deming

Pink dogtooth calcite Missouri: Revere

Pink fans Missouri: Revere

Quartz New Mexico: Deming

Quartz, smoky Missouri: Revere

Pyrite Missouri: Alexandria, Revere

Selenite needles Missouri: Alexandria

Sphalerite Missouri: Alexandria

White barrel calcite Missouri: Revere

Gold (*) Alaska: Fairbanks (3); Arizona: Goldfield; California, Angels Camp (GS), Coloma, Columbia, Jackson, Mariposa, Nevada City, Pine Grove, Placerville; Colorado: Idaho Springs (2); Georgia: Dahlonega (2), Helen; Idaho: Moscow (GS); Indiana: Knightstown; Massachusetts: Athol (Vermont); Montana: Alder (O), Helena; North Carolina: Cherokee, Marion, New London, Stanfield, Union Mills; South Dakota: Deadwood, Keystone, Lead

Goshenite Colorado: Lake George

Goyazite Maine: Poland (GS)

Graftonite Maine: Poland (GS); New Hampshire: Grafton (I)

Gummite New Hampshire: Grafton (I)

Gypsum, curved California: Palo Verde (MM)

Hedenburgite New Mexico: Magdalena

Hematite Montana: Helena; New Mexico: Magdalena

Hemimorphite New Mexico: Bingham

Herderite, hydroxyl Maine: Bethel, Poland (GS), West Paris

Herkimer "diamonds" See Quartz

Heterosite Maine: Poland (GS)

Hiddenite (spodumene) North Carolina: Hiddenite

Hureaylite Maine: Poland (GS)

Iron minerals New Mexico: Magdalena

Iron ore Michigan: Iron Mountain (M)

Jade California: Pine Grove

Jadite Montana: Helena (S)

Jahnsite Maine: Poland (GS)

Jasper Arkansas: Murfreesboro (S); California: Pine Grove; Montana: Helena (S); Oklahoma: Kenton; Oregon: Madras, Yachats; Texas: Alpine
  Brown jasper New Mexico: Deming
  Chocolate jasper New Mexico: Deming
  Orange jasper New Mexico: Deming
  Picture jasper Oregon: Mitchell
  Pink jasper New Mexico: Deming
  Variegated jasper New Mexico: Deming
  Yellow jasper New Mexico: Deming

Jarosite New Mexico: Bingham

Kaolinite Maine: Poland (GS)

Kasolite New Hampshire: Grafton (I)

Kosnarite Maine: Poland (GS)

Kyanite North Carolina (*): Franklin, Little Switzerland

Labradorite Texas: Alpine

Lake County "diamonds" See Quartz

Landsite Maine: Poland (GS)

Laueite Maine: Poland (GS)

Lepidolite Maine: Poland (GS), West Paris; New Mexico: Dixon; North Carolina (*): Little Switzerland
  Lemon Yellow Lepidolite New Hampshire: Grafton (I)

Lepidomelane New Hampshire: Grafton (I)

Linarite New Mexico: Bingham

Lithiophyllite Maine: Poland (GS); New Hampshire: Grafton (I)

Lollingite Maine: Poland (GS)

Ludlamite Maine: Poland (GS)

Magnesium oxide See Psilomellane

Magnesium oxide minerals New Mexico: Deming

Malachite New Mexico: Magdalena; Utah: Moab (GS)

Manganapatite New Hampshire: Grafton (I)

Manganese minerals New Mexico: Deming

Manganese oxide minerals New Mexico: Deming

Marcasite New Hampshire: Grafton (I)

McCrillisite Maine: Poland (GS)

Mica Maine: Poland (GS), West Paris; New Hampshire: Grafton (I); South Dakota: Custer (GS); Virginia: Amelia

Microcline Maine: Poland (GS)

Microlite New Mexico: Dixon

Mitridatite Maine: Poland (GS)

Molybdenite New Hampshire: Grafton

Montebrasite Maine: Poland (GS)

Montmorillonite Maine: Poland (GS), West Paris; New Hampshire: Grafton (I)

Monzaite Maine: Poland (GS)

Moonstone North Carolina (*): Franklin (7), Little Switzerland, Spruce Pine

Moraesite Maine: Poland (GS)

Murdochite New Mexico: Bingham

Muscovite New Hampshire: Grafton (I); New Mexico: Dixon

Opal
    Black opal Nevada: Orovado
    Common opal New Mexico: Deming
    Fire opal Nevada: Gerlach, Orovado
    Hyalite opal Maine: Bethel
    Precious opal Idaho: Spencer; Nevada: Sun Valley (GS); Texas: Alpine
    Wood opal Nevada: Denio

Orthoclase Maine: Poland (GS)

Perhamite Maine: Poland (GS)

Parsonite New Hampshire: Grafton (I)

Perlite (black to gray) New Mexico: Deming

Peridot Arkansas: Murfreesboro (S); North Carolina (*): Franklin

Petalite Maine: Poland (GS), West Paris

Phenakite Virginia: Amelia

Phosphosiderite Maine: Poland (GS)

Phosphouranylite Maine: Poland (GS)

Phosphyanylite New Hampshire: Grafton (I)

Pitch Stone with seams of red & brown New Mexico: Deming

Plattnerite New Mexico: Bingham

Pollucite Maine: Poland (GS), West Paris

Psilomelane New Hampshire: Grafton (I)

Purpurite Maine: Poland (GS); New Hampshire: Grafton (I); South Dakota: Custer (GS)

Pyrite Maine: Bethel, Poland (GS); New Hampshire: Grafton (I); New Mexico: Magdalena; Virginia: Amelia; Washington: Ravensdale (GS)

Pyrrhotite New Hampshire: Grafton (I)

Quartz Arkansas: Hot Springs, Mt. Ida (7) (Y), Murfreesboro (S); California: Pine Grove; Colorado: Lake George; Maine: Poland (GS); Montana: Dillon, Helena (S); New Hampshire: Grafton; New Mexico: Bingham, Deming, Dixon, Socorro (Y); South Dakota: Custer (GS); Texas: Alpine; Virginia: Amelia; Washington: Ravensdale (GS)
   Clear North Carolina (*): Franklin, Hiddenite, Little Switzerland, Spruce Pine
   Milky Maine: Bethel
   Orange Maine: West Paris
   Parallel growth Maine: West Paris
   Pseudocubic crystals Maine: West Paris
   Rose Georgia: Helen (SA); Maine: West Paris; New Hampshire: Grafton (I); North Carolina (*): Franklin, Little Switzerland; South Dakota: Custer (GS)
   Rose (gem quality) Maine: West Paris
   Rutilated North Carolina (*): Little Switzerland, Spruce Pine
   Smoky Georgia: Helen (SA); Maine: Bethel, West Paris; New Hampshire: Grafton (I); North Carolina (*): Almond, Cherokee, Franklin (6), Hiddenite, Little Switzerland (2), Spruce Pine (2)
   Smoky (gem quality) Maine: West Paris

Quartz "diamonds"
   Lake Co. "diamonds" (moon tears) California: Lake County
   Cape May "diamonds" New Jersey: Cape May
   Herkimer "diamonds" New York: Herkimer, Middleville, St. Johnsville

Reddingite Maine: Poland (GS); New Hampshire: Grafton (I)

Rhodochrosite Maine: Poland (GS)

Rhodolite (garnet) North Carolina: Franklin (2)

Rochbridgeite Maine: Poland (GS)

Rose rocks See Barite Rose

Rubies California: Pine Grove; Georgia: Dahlonega (SA); Montana: Helena (R); North Carolina (*): Almond, Cherokee, Franklin (13), Little Switzerland (2), Spruce Pine (3)

Rutile Maine: Bethel, Poland (GS); North Carolina: Franklin (2), Hiddenite; Virginia: Amelia

Safflorite New Hampshire: Grafton (I)

Sapphires Georgia: Dahlonega (SA); Montana: Alder (O), Clinton (GS), Helena (2), Phillipsburg; North Carolina (*): Almond, Canton, Cherokee, Franklin (13), Hiddenite, Little Switzerland (2), Spruce Pine

Scheelite Maine: West Paris

Selenite crystals New Mexico: Bingham; Oklahoma: Jet (Y)

Septarian nodules Utah: Moab (GS)

Serpentine Montana: Helena (S)

Siderite Maine: Bethel

Silica minerals New Mexico: Deming

Sillimanite New Hampshire: Grafton (I); North Carolina (*): Franklin (2), Hiddenite

Smithsonite New Mexico: Bingham, Magdalena, Socorro (Y)

Soddylite (pseudo uranite) New Hampshire: Grafton (I)

Spangolite New Mexico: Bingham

Spessartine New Mexico: Dixon

Spodumene Maine: Poland (GS), West Paris; New Mexico: Dixon
    Altered Spodumene Maine: West Paris
    Hiddenite North Carolina: Hiddenite

Staurolite New Hampshire: Grafton (I); Virginia: Stuart

Stewartite Maine: Poland (GS)

Strunzite Maine: Poland (GS)

Sunstone, Oregon Nevada: Sun Valley (GS)

Switzerite Maine: Poland (GS)

Tantalite-Columbite New Mexico: Dixon; Virginia: Amelia

Tantalum South Dakota: Custer (GS)

Thundereggs New Mexico: Deming; Oregon: Madras, Mitchell

Tobernite New Hampshire: Grafton (I)

Topaz Georgia: Helen (SA); Maine: Poland (GS); Montana: Helena (R); New Hampshire: Grafton (I); North Carolina (SA): Cherokee, Franklin (6), Little Switzerland (3), Spruce Pine (3); Texas: Mason (2); Virginia: Amelia
    Blue topaz Colorado: Lake George
    Blue/sherry bicolor Colorado: Lake George
    Phenakite crystals in topaz Colorado: Lake George (U)
    Pink topaz Washington: Ravensdale (GS)
    Sherry topaz Colorado: Lake George

Torberite Maine: Poland (GS)

Tourmaline Maine: Poland (GS), West Paris; North Carolina (*): Franklin (7), Hiddenite, Little Switzerland (3), Spruce Pine (3) (FT); South Dakota, Custer (GS); Virginia: Amelia

Black tourmaline Maine: Bethel, Poland (GS), West Paris; New Hampshire: Grafton (I)

Gem tourmaline Maine: West Paris

Green tourmaline Maine: West Paris

Triphyllite Maine: Poland (GS), West Paris; New Hampshire: Grafton (I)

Triplite Maine: Poland (GS)

Turquoise Nevada: Sun Valley (GS)

Uralolite Maine: Poland (GS)

Uranite Maine: Poland (GS); New Hampshire: Grafton (I) (Species with gummite—world-famous)

Uranium minerals New Hampshire: Grafton (I)

Uranophane New Hampshire: Grafton (I)

Vandendriesscheite New Hampshire: Grafton (I)

Vesuvianite Maine: Poland (GS), West Paris (2)

Vivianite New Hampshire: Grafton (I)

Voelerkenite New Hampshire: Grafton (I)

Wardilite Maine: Poland (GS)

Whitlockite Maine: Poland (GS)

Whitmoreite Maine: Poland (GS)

Wodginite Maine: Poland (GS)

Wulfenite New Mexico: Bingham

Zircon Maine: Bethel, Poland (GS), West Paris; New Hampshire: Grafton (I)

Annual Events

JANUARY

Quartzite, AZ, Gem and Mineral Shows—Mid-January–mid-February

FEBRUARY

Tucson, AZ, Gem and Mineral Show—First two weeks in February

MARCH

Scottsdale, AZ, Minerals of Arizona Symposium—1 day in March each year, sponsored by the Arizona Mineral & Mining Museum Foundation and the Arizona Department of Mines & Mineral Resources

Boron, CA, Rock Bonanza—Weekend before easter

Socorro, NM, Rockhounding Days in Socorro County—Last weekend in March

APRIL

Alpine, TX, Alpine Gem Show—Mid-April

Franklin, NJ, The New Jersey Earth Science Association Gem and Mineral Show and Outdoor Swap & Sell—Late April

MAY

Cherokee, OK, The Crystal Festival and Selenite Crystal Dig—First Saturday in May

Noble, OK, Rose Rock Festival—First Saturday in May

Augusta, ME, Maine Mineral Symposium—Third weekend in May

University Park, PA, Mineral Symposium c/o Penn State Mineral Museum—3 days in May

JUNE

Prineville, OR, Rockhounds Pow-Wow—Mid-June

Casper, WY, Tate Geological Museum Symposium on Wyoming Geology—June

JULY

Franklin, NC, Macon County Gemboree—Third weekend in July

Cottage Grove, OR, Bohemia Mining Days—Four days in July

AUGUST

Spruce Pine, NC, Original North Carolina Mineral and Gem Festival—Four days at the beginning of August

Pittsburgh, PA, Carnegie Museum of Natural History Gem and Mineral Show—Last weekend in August

SEPTEMBER

No information available.

OCTOBER

Coloma, CA, Marshall Gold Discovery State Park Gold Rush Days—End of September–beginning of October

Jasper, GA, Pickens County Marble Festival—First weekend in October

Mt. Ida, AR, Quartz Crystal Festival and World Championship Dig—Second weekend in October

Franklin, NC, "Leaf Looker" Gemboree—Second weekend in October

NOVEMBER

No information available.

DECEMBER

No information available.

State Gem and Mineral Symbols

STATE	GEMSTONE	MINERAL	STONE/ROCK
Alabama	Star Blue Quartz (1990)	Hematite (1967)	Marble (1969)
Alaska	Jade (1968)	Gold (1968)	
Arizona	Turquoise (1974)		
Arkansas	Diamond	Quartz	Bauxite
California	Benitoite	Gold	Serpentine (1965)
Colorado	Aquamarine (1971)		
Connecticut	Garnet (1977)		
Delaware		Sillimanite	
Florida	Moonstone		Agatized coral
Georgia	Quartz	Staurolite	
Hawaii	Black Coral		
Idaho	Star Garnet (1967)		
Illinois		Fluorite (1965)	
Indiana			Limestone
Iowa			Geode
Kansas			
Kentucky	Freshwater Pearl		
Louisiana	Agate		
Maine		Tourmaline (1971)	
Maryland			
Massachusetts	Rhodonite	Babingtonite	Plymouth Rock, Dighton Rock, Roxbury Conglomerate
Michigan	Isle Royal Greenstone (Chlorostrolite) (1972)		Petosky Stone (1965)
Minnesota	Lake Superior Agate		
Mississippi			Petrified Wood (1976)
Missouri		Galena (1967)	Mozarkite (1967)

STATE	GEMSTONE	MINERAL	STONE/ROCK
Montana			Sapphire & Agate (1969)
Nebraska	Blue Agate (1967)		Prairie Agate (1967)
Nevada	Virgin Valley Blackfire Opal (1987) (Precious) Turquoise (1987) (Semiprecious)	Silver	Sandstone (1987)
New Hampshire	Smoky Quartz	Beryl	Granite
New Jersey			
New Mexico	Turquoise (1967)		
New York	Garnet (1969)		
North Carolina	Emerald (1973)		
North Dakota			
Ohio	Flint (1965)		
Oklahoma			Barite Rose
Oregon	Sunstone (1987)		Thundereggs (1965)
Pennsylvania			
Rhode Island	Bowenite		Cumberlandite
South Carolina	Amethyst		Blue Granite
South Dakota	Fairburn Agate (1966)	Rose Quartz (1966) (Mineral/Stone)	
Tennessee	Tennessee River Pearls		Limestone and Tennessee Marble
Texas	Texas Blue Topaz (1969) Lone Star Cut (1977) (Gemstone Cut)		Petrified Palmwood (1960)
Utah	Topaz		
Vermont			
Virginia			
Washington	Petrified Wood (1975)		
West Virginia			
Wisconsin		Galena (1971)	Red Granite (1971)
Wyoming	Nephrite Jade (1967)		

Finding Your Own Birthstone

Following is a listing of fee dig sites presented in this four-volume guide where you can find your birthstone! Refer to the individual mine listings for more information on individual mines.

Garnet (January Birthstone) Georgia: Dahlonega (SA), Helen (SA); Idaho: St. Maries; Maine: Bethel, Poland (GS), West Paris (3); Montana: Alder, Helena (S); New Hampshire: Grafton (I); New Mexico: Dixon; North Carolina (*): Almond, Cherokee, Franklin (7), Hiddenite, Little Switzerland (2), Spruce Pine (3) (FT); Nevada, Ely; Washington: Ravensdale (GS)
Almandine garnets Maine: Poland (GS); Nevada, Ely
Pyrope garnets North Carolina: Franklin
Rhodolite garnets North Carolina: Franklin (5)

Amethyst (February Birthstone) Arkansas: Murfreesboro(S); Georgia: Helen (SA); Maine: Bethel (R), West Paris; Montana: Dillon; Nevada: Sun Valley (GS) (crystal scepters); New Hampshire: Grafton (I); New Mexico: Bingham; North Carolina (*): Cherokee, Franklin (5), Little Switzerland, Spruce Pine (3)

Aquamarine or Bloodstone (March Birthstone):
Aquamarine Maine: Bethel, Poland (GS); New Hampshire: Grafton (I); North Carolina (*): Hiddenite, Little Switzerland (5), Spruce Pine (2) (FT)
Brushy Creek Aq. North Carolina: Spruce Pine (FT)
Weisman Aq. North Carolina: Spruce Pine (FT)
Bloodstone No listing

Diamond (April Birthstone) Arkansas: Murfreesboro

Emerald (May Birthstone) Georgia: Dahlonega (SA); North Carolina (*): Cherokee, Franklin, Hiddenite, Little Switzerland (2), Spruce Pine (2)
Crabtree Emerald North Carolina: Spruce Pine

Moonstone or Pearl (June Birthstone):
Moonstone North Carolina (*): Franklin (7), Little Switzerland, Spruce Pine
Pearl No listing

Ruby (July Birthstone) Georgia: Dahlonega (SA); Montana: Helena (R); North Carolina (*): Cherokee, Franklin (13), Little Switzerland (2), Spruce Pine (3)
Peridot or Sardonyx (August Birthstone):
Peridot Arkansas: Murfreesboro (S); North Carolina (*): Franklin

Sardonyx No listing

Sapphire (September Birthstone) Georgia: Dahlonega (SA); Montana: Alder (O), Clinton (GS), Helena (2), Phillipsburg; North Carolina (*): Canton, Cherokee, Franklin (13), Hiddenite, Little Switzerland (2), Spruce Pine

Opal or Tourmaline (October Birthstone):
Opal
    Black opal Nevada: Orovado
    Common opal New Mexico: Deming
    Fire opal Nevada: Gerlach, Orovado
    Hyalite opal Maine: Bethel
    Precious opal Idaho: Spencer; Nevada: Sun Valley (GS); Texas: Alpine
    Wood opal Nevada: Denio
Tourmaline Maine: Poland (GS), West Paris; North Carolina (*): Franklin (7), Hiddenite, Little Switzerland (3), Spruce Pine (3) (FT); South Dakota, Custer (GS); Virginia: Amelia
    Black tourmaline Maine: Bethel, Poland (GS), West Paris; New Hampshire: Grafton (I)
    Gem tourmaline Maine: West Paris
    Green tourmaline Maine: West Paris

Topaz (November Birthstone) Georgia: Helen (SA); Maine: Poland (GS); Montana: Helena (R); New Hampshire: Grafton (I); North Carolina (SA): Cherokee, Franklin (6), Little Switzerland (3), Spruce Pine (3); Texas: Mason (2); Virginia: Amelia
    Blue topaz Colorado: Lake George
    Blue/sherry bicolor Colorado: Lake George
    Phenakitite in topaz crystals Colorado: Lake George (U)
    Pink topaz Washington: Ravensdale (GS)
    Sherry topaz Colorado: Lake George

Turquoise or Lapis Lazuli (December Birthstone):
Turquoise Nevada: Sun Valley (GS)
Lapis Lazuli No listing

The preceding list of birthstones is taken from a list adopted in 1912 by the American National Association of Jewelers ("The Evolution of Birthstones" from *Jewelry & Gems—The Buying Guide* by Antoinette L. Matlins and A.C. Bonanno; Gemstone Press, 1997).

Finding Your Anniversary Stone

The following is a listing of fee dig sites contained in this four-volume guide where you can find the stone that is associated with a particular anniversary.

First: Gold (Jewelry) Alaska: Fairbanks (3); Arizona: Goldfield; California, Angels Camp (GS), Coloma, Columbia, Jackson, Mariposa, Nevada City, Pine Grove, Placerville; Colorado: Idaho Springs (2); Georgia: Dahlonega (2), Helen; Idaho: Moscow (GS); Indiana: Knightstown; Massachusetts: Athol (Vermont); Montana: Alder (O), Helena; North Carolina: Cherokee, Marion, New London, Stanfield, Union Mills; South Dakota: Deadwood, Keystone, Lead

Second: Garnet Georgia: Dahlonega (SA), Helen (SA); Idaho: St. Maries; Maine: Bethel, Poland (GS), West Paris (3); Montana: Alder, Helena (S); New Hampshire: Grafton (I); New Mexico: Dixon; North Carolina (*): Almond, Cherokee, Franklin (7), Hiddenite, Little Switzerland (2), Spruce Pine (3) (FT); Nevada, Ely; Washington: Ravensdale (GS)
  Almandine garnets Maine: Poland (GS); Nevada, Ely
  Pyrope garnets North Carolina: Franklin
  Rhodolite garnets North Carolina: Franklin (5)

Third: Pearl No listing

Fourth: Blue Topaz Colorado: Lake George

Fifth: Sapphire Georgia: Dahlonega (SA); Montana: Alder (O), Clinton (GS), Helena (2), Phillipsburg; North Carolina (*): Almond, Canton, Cherokee, Franklin (13), Hiddenite, Little Switzerland (2), Spruce Pine

Sixth: Amethyst Arkansas: Murfreesboro (S); Georgia: Helen (SA); Maine: Bethel (R), West Paris; Montana: Dillon; Nevada: Sun Valley (GS) (crystal scepters); New Hampshire: Grafton (I); New Mexico: Bingham; North Carolina (*): Cherokee, Franklin (5), Little Switzerland, Spruce Pine (3)

Seventh: Onyx No listing

Eighth: Tourmaline Maine: Poland (GS), West Paris; North Carolina (*): Franklin (7), Hiddenite, Little Switzerland (3), Spruce Pine (3) (FT); South Dakota, Custer (GS); Virginia: Amelia
  Black tourmaline Maine: Bethel, Poland (GS), West Paris, New Hampshire: Grafton (I)
  Gem tourmaline Maine: West Paris
  Green tourmaline Maine: West Paris

Ninth: Lapis Lazuli No listing

Tenth: Diamond (Jewelry) Arkansas: Murfreesboro

Eleventh: Turquoise Nevada: Sun Valley (GS)

Twelfth: Jade No listing

Thirteenth: Citrine Georgia: Helen (SA); North Carolina (SA): Almond, Cherokee, Franklin (5), Little Switzerland, Spruce Pine (3)

Fourteenth: Opal
Black opal Nevada: Orovado
Common opal New Mexico: Deming
Fire opal Nevada: Gerlach, Orovado;
Hyalite opal Maine: Bethel
Precious opal Idaho: Spencer; Nevada: Sun Valley (GS); Texas: Alpine
Wood opal Nevada: Denio

Fifteenth: Ruby California: Pine Grove; Georgia: Dahlonega (SA); Montana: Helena (R); North Carolina (*): Almond, Cherokee, Franklin (13), Little Switzerland (2), Spruce Pine (3)

Twentieth: Emerald Georgia: Dahlonega (SA); North Carolina (*): Cherokee, Franklin (1), Hiddenite, Little Switzerland (4), Spruce Pine (2) (also crabtree emerald)

Twenty-fifth: Silver No listing

Thirtieth: Pearl No listing

Thirty-fifth: Emerald Georgia: Dahlonega (SA); North Carolina (*): Cherokee, Franklin, Hiddenite, Little Switzerland (2), Spruce Pine (2) (also crabree emerald)

Fortieth: Ruby California: Pine Grove; Georgia: Dahlonega (SA); Montana: Helena (R); North Carolina (*): Almond, Cherokee, Franklin (13), Little Switzerland (2), Spruce Pine (3)

Forty-fifth: Sapphire Georgia: Dahlonega (SA); Montana: Alder, Clinton (GS), Helena (2), Phillipsburg; North Carolina (*): Almond, Canton, Cherokee, Franklin (13), Hiddenite, Little Switzerland (2), Spruce Pine

Fiftieth: Gold Alaska: Fairbanks (3); Arizona: Goldfield; California, Angels Camp, Coloma, Columbia, Jackson, Mariposa, Nevada City, Pine Grove, Placerville; Colorado: Idaho Springs (2); Georgia: Dahlonega (2), Helen; Idaho: Moscow (GS); Indiana: Knightstown; Massachusetts: Athol (Vermont); Montana: Alder (O), Helena; North Carolina: Cherokee, Marion, New London, Stanfield, Union Mills; South Dakota: Deadwood, Keystone, Lead

Fifty-fifth: Alexandrite No listing

Sixtieth: Diamond Arkansas: Murfreesboro

Finding Your Zodiac Stone

The following is a listing of fee dig sites contained in this four-volume guide where you can find the stone that is associated with a particular zodiac sign. Refer to the individual mine listings for more information.

Aquarius (January 21–February 21) Garnet Georgia: Dahlonega (SA), Helen (SA); Idaho: St. Maries; Maine: Bethel, Poland (GS), West Paris (3); Montana: Alder, Helena (S); New Hampshire: Grafton (I); New Mexico: Dixon; North Carolina (*): Almond, Cherokee, Franklin (7), Hiddenite, Little Switzerland (2), Spruce Pine (3) (FT); Nevada, Ely; Washington: Ravensdale (GS)
  Almandine garnets Maine: Poland (GS); Nevada, Ely
  Pyrope garnets North Carolina: Franklin
  Rhodolite garnets North Carolina: Franklin (5)

Pisces (February 22–March 21) Amethyst Arkansas: Murfreesboro (S); Georgia: Helen (SA); Maine: Bethel (R), West Paris; Montana: Dillon; Nevada: Sun Valley (GS) (crystal scepters); New Hampshire: Grafton (I); New Mexico: Bingham; North Carolina (*): Almond, Cherokee, Franklin (5), Little Switzerland, Spruce Pine (3)

Aries (March 21–April 20) Bloodstone (green chalcedony with red spots) No listing

Taurus (April 21–May 21) Sapphire Georgia: Dahlonega (SA); Montana: Alder (O), Clinton (GS), Helena (2), Phillipsburg; North Carolina (*): Almond, Canton, Cherokee, Franklin (13), Hiddenite, Little Switzerland (2), Spruce Pine

Gemini (May 22–June 21) Agate Arkansas: Murfreesboro(S); Iowa: Bonaporte; Montana: Helena (S); Nevada: Gerlach; New Mexico: Deming (GS); Oklahoma: Kenton (2); Oregon: Yachats; South Dakota: Wall; Texas: Three Rivers; Utah: Moab (GS); Virginia: Amelia
  Banded agate Texas: Alpine
  Fire agate California: Palo Verde
  Iris agate Texas: Alpine
  Ledge agate Oregon: Madras
  Moss agate Oregon: Madras, Mitchell; Texas: Alpine (2), Wyoming: Shell
  Polka-dot jasp-agate Oregon: Madras
  Plume agate Oregon: Madras
  Pompom agate Texas: Alpine
  Rainbow agate Oregon: Madras
  Red plume agate Texas: Alpine

Cancer (June 22–July 22) Emerald Georgia: Dahlonega (SA); North Carolina (*):

Cherokee, Franklin, Hiddenite, Little Switzerland (2), Spruce Pine (2)

Crabtree emerald North Carolina: Spruce Pine

Leo (July 23–August 22) Onyx No listing

Virgo (August 23–September 22) Carnelian No listing

Libra (September 23–October 23) Chrysolite or Peridot:
Peridot Arkansas: Murfreesboro (S); North Carolina (*): Franklin

Scorpio (October 24–November 21) Beryl Maine: Poland (GS), West Paris; New Mexico, Dixon; North Carolina (*): Little Switzerland (2), Spruce Pine (2); South Dakota: Custer (GS); Virginia: Amelia (2)
Aqua beryl New Hampshire: Grafton (I)
Blue beryl New Hampshire: Grafton (I)
Golden beryl North Carolina: Spruce Pine (FT); New Hampshire: Grafton (I)

Sagittarius (November 22–December 21) Topaz Georgia: Helen (SA); Maine: Poland (GS); Montana: Helena (R); New Hampshire: Grafton (I); North Carolina (SA): Cherokee, Franklin (6), Little Switzerland (3), Spruce Pine (3); Texas: Mason (2); Virginia: Amelia
Blue topaz Colorado: Lake George
Blue/sherry bicolor Colorado: Lake George
Phenakitite crystals in topaz Colorado: Lake George (U)
Pink topaz Washington: Ravensdale (GS)
Sherry topaz Colorado: Lake George

Capricorn (December 22–January 21) Ruby California: Pine Grove; Georgia: Dahlonega (SA); Montana: Helena (R); North Carolina (*): Almond, Cherokee, Franklin (13), Little Switzerland (2), Spruce Pine (3)

The preceding list of zodiacal stones has been passed on from an early Hindu legend (taken from *Jewelry & Gems—The Buying Guide* by Antoinette L. Matlins and A.C. Bonanno, Gemstone Press, 1997).

The following is an old Spanish list, probably representing Arab traditions, which ascribes the following stones to various signs of the zodiac (taken from *Jewelry & Gems—The Buying Guide* by Antoinette L. Matlins and A.C. Bonanno, Gemstone Press, 1997).

Aquarius (January 21–February 21) Amethyst Arkansas: Murfreesboro (S); Georgia: Helen (SA); Maine: Bethel (R), West Paris; Montana: Dillon; New Hampshire: Grafton (I); New Mexico: Bingham; North Carolina (*): Almond, Cherokee, Franklin (5), Little Switzerland, Spruce Pine (3)
Crystal scepters Nevada: Sun Valley (GS)

Pisces (February 22–March 21) Undistinguishable

Aries (March 21–April 20) Quartz Arkansas: Hot Springs, Mt. Ida (7) (Y), Murfreesboro (S); California: Pine Grove; Colorado: Lake George; Maine: Poland (GS); Montana: Dillon, Helena; New Hampshire: Grafton; New Mexico: Bingham, Deming, Dixon, Socorro (Y); South Dakota: Custer (GS); Texas: Alpine; Virginia: Amelia; Washington: Ravensdale (GS)
 Clear North Carolina (*): Franklin, Hiddenite, Little Switzerland, Spruce Pine
 Milky Maine: Bethel
 Orange Maine: West Paris
 Parallel growth Maine: West Paris
 Pseudocubic crystals Maine: West Paris
 Rose Georgia: Helen (SA); Maine: West Paris; New Hampshire: Grafton (I); North Carolina (*): Franklin), Little Switzerland; South Dakota: Custer (GS)
 Rose (gem quality) Maine: West Paris
 Rutilated North Carolina (*): Little Switzerland, Spruce Pine
 Smoky Georgia: Helen (SA); Maine: Bethel, West Paris; New Hampshire: Grafton (I); North Carolina (*): Almond, Cherokee, Franklin (6),Hiddenite, Little Switzerland (2), Spruce Pine (2)
 Smoky (gem quality) Maine: West Paris

Quartz "diamonds"
 Lake Co. "diamonds" (moon tears) California: Lake County
 Cape May "diamonds" New Jersey: Cape May
 Herkimer "diamonds" New York: Herkimer, Middleville, St. Johnsville

Taurus (April 21–May 21) Rubies, Diamonds:
Rubies California: Pine Grove; Georgia: Dahlonega (SA); Montana: Helena (R); North Carolina (*): Almond, Cherokee, Franklin (13), Little Switzerland (2), Spruce Pine (3)
Diamonds Arkansas: Murfreesboro

Gemini (May 22–June 21) Sapphire Georgia: Dahlonega (SA); Montana: Alder (O), Clinton (GS), Helena (2), Phillipsburg; North Carolina (*): Almond, Canton, Cherokee, Franklin (13), Hiddenite, Little Switzerland (2), Spruce Pine

Cancer (June 22–July 22) Agate and Beryl:
Agate Arkansas: Murfreesboro (S); Iowa: Bonaporte; Montana: Helena (S); Nevada: Gerlach; New Mexico: Deming (GS); Oklahoma: Kenton (2); Oregon: Yachats; South Dakota: Wall; Texas: Three Rivers; Utah: Moab (GS); Virginia: Amelia
 Banded agate Texas: Alpine
 Fire agate California: Palo Verde
 Iris agate Texas: Alpine
 Ledge agate Oregon: Madras
 Moss agate Oregon: Madras, Mitchell; Texas: Alpine (2), Wyoming: Shell
 Polka-dot agate Oregon: Madras (R)
 Plume agate Oregon: Madras
 Pompom agate Texas: Alpine

Rainbow agate Oregon: Madras (R)
Red plume agate Texas: Alpine
Beryl Maine: Poland (GS), West Paris; New Mexico, Dixon; North Carolina (*): Little Switzerland (2), Spruce Pine (2); South Dakota: Custer (GS); Virginia: Amelia (2)
 Aqua beryl New Hampshire: Grafton (I)
 Blue beryl New Hampshire: Grafton (I)
 Golden beryl North Carolina: Spruce Pine (FT); New Hampshire: Grafton (I)

Leo (July 23–August 22) Topaz Georgia: Helen (SA); Maine: Poland (GS); Montana: Helena (R); New Hampshire: Grafton (I); North Carolina (SA): Cherokee, Franklin (6), Little Switzerland (3), Spruce Pine (3); Texas: Mason (2); Virginia: Amelia
 Blue topaz Colorado: Lake George
 Blue/sherry bicolor Colorado: Lake George
 Phenakitite crystals in topaz Colorado: Lake George (U)
 Pink topaz Washington: Ravensdale (GS)
 Sherry topaz Colorado: Lake George

Virgo (August 23–September 22) Bloodstone (green chalcedony with red spots)
 No listing

Libra (September 23–October 23) Jasper Arkansas: Murfreesboro (S); California: Pine Grove; Montana: Helena; Oklahoma: Kenton; Oregon: Madras, Yachats; Texas: Alpine
 Brown jasper New Mexico: Deming
 Chocolate jasper New Mexico: Deming
 Orange jasper New Mexico: Deming
 Picture jasper Oregon: Mitchell
 Pink jasper New Mexico: Deming
 Variegated jasper New Mexico: Deming
 Yellow jasper New Mexico: Deming

Scorpio (October 24–November 21) Garnet Georgia: Dahlonega (SA), Helen (SA); Idaho: St. Maries; Maine: Bethel, Poland (GS), West Paris (3); Montana: Alder, Helena (S); New Hampshire: Grafton (I); New Mexico: Dixon; North Carolina (*): Almond, Cherokee, Franklin (7), Hiddenite, Little Switzerland (2), Spruce Pine (3) (FT); Nevada, Ely; Washington: Ravensdale (GS)
 Almandine garnets Maine: Poland (GS); Nevada, Ely
 Pyrope garnets North Carolina: Franklin
 Rhodolite garnets North Carolina: Franklin (5)

Sagittarius (November 22–December 21) Emerald Georgia: Dahlonega (SA); North Carolina (*): Cherokee, Franklin, Hiddenite, Little Switzerland (2), Spruce Pine (2)
Crabtree emerald North Carolina: Spruce Pine

Capricorn (December 22–January 21) Chalcedony New Mexico: Deming
Blue chalcedony Nevada: Sun Valley (GS)

Some Publications on Gems and Minerals

Lapidary Journal

60 Chestnut Avenue
Suite 201
Devon, PA 19333-1312
Phone: (610) 293-1112
Fax 293-1717
E-mail: ljmagazine@aol.com
www.lapidaryjournal.com

Rock & Mineral

5341 Thrasher Dr.
Cincinnati, OH 45247
Phone: (513) 574-7142 or (800)
365-9753
Fax: 574-7142
E-mail: rocks&minerals@fuse.net
www.heldref.org
www.mineralart.com/rocks_and_
minerals

Rock & Gem

c/o Miller Magazines, Inc.
4880 Market Street
Ventura, CA 93003-7783
Phone: (805) 644-3824
www.rockhounds.com

Gold Prospector

Gold Prospectors Association of
America, Inc.
43445 Business Park Drive
Suite 113
Temecula, CA 92590
Phone: (800) 551-9707
www.goldprospectors.org

Send Us Your Feedback

Disclaimer

The authors have made every reasonable effort to obtain accurate information for this guide. However, much of the information in the book is based on material provided by the sites and has not been verified independently. The information given here does not represent recommendations, but merely a listing of information. The authors and publisher accept no liability for any accident or loss incurred when readers are patronizing the establishments listed herein. The authors and publisher accept no liability for errors or omissions. Since sites may shut down or change their hours of operations or fees without advance notice, please call the site before your visit for confirmation before planning your trip.

The authors would appreciate being informed of changes, additions, or deletions that should be made to this guide. To that end, a form is attached, which can be filled out and mailed to the authors for use in future editions of the guide.

Have We Missed Your Mine or Museum?

This is a project with a national scope, based on extensive literature search, phone and mail inquiry, and personal investigation. However, we are dealing with a business in which many owners are retiring or closing and selling their sites. In addition, many of the mines, guide services, and smaller museums have limited publicity, known more by word of mouth than by publication. Thus, it is possible that an operation was not included in this guide. Please let us know if you own or operate a mine, guide service, or museum, or have visited a mine, guide service, or museum that is not in the guide. It will be considered for inclusion in the next edition of the guide. Send updates to:

Treasure Hunter's Guides
GemStone Press
Route 4, Sunset Farm Offices
P.O. Box 237
Woodstock, VT 05091

Do You Have a Rockhounding Story to Share?

If you have a special story about a favorite dig site, send it in for consideration for use in the next edition of the guide.

A Request to Mines and Museums:

For sites already included in this guide, we request that you put us on your annual mailing list so that we may have an updated copy of your information.

Notes on Museums

In this guide we have included listings of museums with noteworthy gem, mineral, or rock collections. We particularly tried to find local museums displaying gems or minerals native to the area where they are located. This list is by no means complete, and if you feel we missed an important listing, let us know by completing the following form. Since these guides focus specifically on gems and minerals, only those exhibits have been recognized in the museum listings, and we do not mention any collection or exhibits of fossils. See our sequel on fossils for information on fossil collections.

READER'S CONTRIBUTION

I would like to supply the following information for possible inclusion in the next edition of *The Treasure Hunter's Guide*:

Type of entry: ☐ fee dig   ☐ guide service   ☐ museum   ☐ mine tour
☐ annual event

This is a: ☐ new entry   ☐ entry currently in the guide

Nature of info: ☐ addition   ☐ change   ☐ deletion

Please describe (brochure and additional info may be attached):

_____

_____

_____

_____

Please supply the following in case we need to contact you regarding your information:

Name: _____

Address: _____

_____

_____

Phone: ( ) _____

E-mail: _____

Date: _____

FIELD NOTES

FIELD NOTES

FIELD NOTES

FIELD NOTES

FIELD NOTES

FIELD NOTES

FIELD NOTES

Identify Your Treasure...
Buy Your Tools and Accessories Directly from GemStone Press

Whatever you need to identify your treasure, GemStone Press can help.
Use this convenient order form, or contact us directly for assistance.

Item/Quantity	Price Ea.*	Total $

Loupes—Professional Jeweler's 10X Triplet Loupes

	Price Ea.*	Total $
_____ Bausch & Lomb 10X Triplet Loupe	$44.00	$ _____
_____ Standard 10X Triplet Loupe	$29.00	_____
_____ The FillFinder™ Darkfield Loupe (RosGem)	$174.95	_____

—Spot filled diamonds, other enhancements and zoning instantly.
Operates with large maglite (optional—see over)

Complete Pocket Instrument Set
SPECIAL SAVINGS!
BUY THIS ESSENTIAL TRIO AND SAVE 12%
Used together, you can identify 85% of all gems with these three portable,
pocket-sized instruments—the essential trio.

• 10X Triplet Loupe • Chelsea Filter • Calcite Dichroscope

Pocket Instrument Set:
Standard: With Standard 10X Loupe • OPL Dichroscope • Chelsea Filter **only $144.95**
Deluxe: With Bausch & Lomb 10X Loupe • Premium Dichroscope • Chelsea Filter **only $179.95**

Color Filters

	Price Ea.*	Total $
_____ Chelsea Filter	$44.95	_____
_____ Synthetic Emerald Filter Set	$32.00	_____
_____ Bead Buyer's & Parcel Picker's Filter Set	$24.00	_____

Pocket Instrument Sets

	Price Ea.*	Total $
_____ **Standard:** With Standard 10X Loupe • OPL Dichroscope • Chelsea Filter	$144.95	_____
_____ **Deluxe:** With Bausch & Lomb 10X Loupe • Premium Dichroscope • Chelsea Filter	$179.95	_____

Calcite Dichroscopes

	Price Ea.*	Total $
_____ Dichroscope (Premium)	$115.00	_____
_____ Dichroscope (OPL)	$89.95	_____

Diamond Testers and Tweezers

	Price Ea.*	Total $
_____ Diamond Star I Diamond Tester	$99.95	_____
_____ Diamond Beam II Diamond Tester	$169.00	_____
_____ Moissketeer 2000 SD	$269.00	_____
_____ Diamond Tweezers/Locking	$10.65	_____
_____ Diamond Tweezers/Non-Locking	$7.80	_____

Gem Analyzer

	Price Ea.*	Total $
_____ Combines Darkfield Loupe, Polariscope and Immersion Cell in "pocket size" unit (RosGem)	$275.00	_____

Jewelry Cleaners

	Price Ea.*	Total $
_____ Ionic Cleaner—Home size model	$59.95	_____
_____ Ionic Cleaner—Professional large size model	$125.00	_____
_____ Ionic Solution—16 oz. bottle	$20.00	_____

See Over for More Instruments & Order Form

* Prices, manufacturing specifications, and terms subject to change without notice. Orders accepted subject to availability.

Discover and Identify Your Treasure...
Buy Your Tools and Accessories Directly from GemStone Press

Item/Quantity	Price Ea.*	Total $

Polariscope
_____ Portable Polariscope — $90.00 — _____

Refractometer
_____ Portable Refractometer (RosGem RFA 322) — $470.00 — _____
  —Operates with small maglite (optional—see below)
_____ Refractive Index Liquid—10 gram — $42.50 — _____

Spectroscopes
_____ Spectroscope—Pocket size model (OPL) — $89.00 — _____
_____ Spectroscope—Desk Model w/stand (OPL) — $225.00 — _____

Ultraviolet Lamps
_____ Small LW/SW — $69.00 — _____
_____ Large LW/SW — $189.00 — _____
_____ Viewing Cabinet (for Large Lamp) — $147.00 — _____
_____ **Purchase Large Lamp & Cabinet together** — $299.00 — _____
  for $299 and save $37.00

Maglites
_____ Large Maglite — $15.00 — _____
_____ Small Maglite — $11.00 — _____

Shipping/Insurance per order in the U.S.: $4.95 1st item, $3.00 each add'l item; $7.95 total for pocket instrument set. Outside the U.S.: Please specify *insured* shipping method you prefer and provide a credit card number for payment. $ _____

TOTAL $_____ *

Check enclosed for $ _____ (Payable to: GEMSTONE Press)
Charge my credit card: ❑ Visa ❑ MasterCard
Name on card _____
Cardholder Address: Street _____
City/State/Zip _____
Credit Card # _____ Exp. Date _____
Signature _____ Phone (_____)_____
Please send to: ❑ Same as Above ❑ Address Below
Name _____
Street _____
City/State/Zip _____ Phone (_____)_____

Phone, mail, or fax orders to:
GEMSTONE Press, Sunset Farm Offices, Route 4, P.O. Box 237, Woodstock, VT 05091
Tel: (802) 457-4000 • Fax: (802) 457-4004 • Credit Card Orders: (800) 962-4544
www.gemstonepress.com
Generous Discounts on Quantity Orders

See Over for More Instruments

TOTAL SATISFACTION GUARANTEE
If for any reason you're not completely delighted with your purchase, return it in resellable condition within 30 days for a full refund.

*All orders must be prepaid by credit card, money order or check in U.S. funds drawn on a U.S. bank.

Prices, manufacturing specifications, and terms subject to change without notice. Orders accepted subject to availability.

014

The "Unofficial Bible" for the Gem & Jewelry Buyer

JEWELRY & GEMS: THE BUYING GUIDE
4TH EDITION

How to Buy Diamonds, Pearls, Colored Gemstones, Gold & Jewelry with Confidence and Knowledge

by Antoinette L. Matlins, PG *and* A.C. Bonanno, FGA, ASA, MGA
—*over 175,000 copies in print*—

Learn the tricks of the trade from *insiders:*

How to buy diamonds, pearls, precious and other popular colored gems with confidence and knowledge. More than just a buying guide . . . discover what's available and what choices you have, what determines quality as well as cost, how to care for and protect valuable gems, what questions to ask before you buy and what to get in writing. Easy to read and understand. Excellent for staff training.

NEW Expanded & Updated Retail Price Guides

Also included:
- How to buy diamonds with confidence
- Determining value in colored gems and pearls
- Important advice for **before and after** you buy
- Over 100 color photos showing dazzling gems, the newest cuts and beautiful classic and contemporary jewelry by award-winning designers
- Special sections:
  - **DESIGN & STYLE** covers classic and innovative settings, tips on getting a larger look and how to get what you want within your budget
  - **GOLD & PLATINUM** covers everything you need to know about gold and platinum: colors, finishes, factors affecting cost, underkarating
  - **PEARLS** covers cultured versus imitation pearls, varieties available, factors affecting value, how to evaluate quality
- Full coverage of exciting new gems recently discovered—"red emerald," neon tourmaline, sunstone and more
- How to properly read diamond grading reports and colored gem reports
- New treatments—and deceptions—and how to guard against them

6" x 9", 304 pp., 16 full-color pages & over 200 color and b/w illustrations/photos
Quality Paperback, ISBN 0-943763-22-3 **$17.95;** HC, ISBN 0-943763-19-3 **$24.95**

FOR CREDIT CARD ORDERS CALL 800-962-4544
Available from your bookstore or directly from the publisher. TRY YOUR BOOKSTORE FIRST.

- -

Please send me **Jewelry & Gems: The Buying Guide:** ____ copies at $17.95 (pb);
___ copies at $24.95 (hc), plus $3.50 s/h for 1st book, $2.00 ea. add'l book in U.S.*
Check enclosed for $_____ (Payable to: GEMSTONE Press)
Charge my credit card: ❏ Visa ❏ MasterCard
Name on card _____
Cardholder Address: Street _____
City/State/Zip _____
Credit Card # _____ Exp. Date _____
Signature _____ Phone (_____)_____
Please send to: ❏ Same as Above ❏ Address Below
Name _____
Street _____
City/State/Zip _____ Phone (_____)_____

TOTAL SATISFACTION GUARANTEE

If for any reason you're not completely delighted with your purchase, return it in resellable condition within 30 days for a full refund.

Phone, mail, or fax orders to: GEMSTONE **Press**, Sunset Farm Offices, Rte. 4
P.O. Box 237, Woodstock, VT 05091 • Tel: (802) 457-4000 • Fax: (802) 457-4004
Credit Card Orders: (800) 962-4544 • **www.gemstonepress.com**
Generous Discounts on Quantity Orders
(Outside U.S.: Specify shipping method (insured) and provide a credit card number for payment.)

Prices subject to change   014

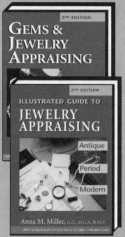

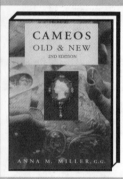

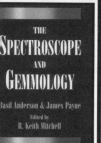